En·tre·pre·neur·ship *for* the Rest of Us

En·tre· pre·neur· ship *for* the Rest of Us

How to Create **INNOVATION** and **OPPORTUNITY** Everywhere

Paul B. Brown

First published by Bibliomotion, Inc.
39 Harvard Street
Brookline, MA 02445
Tel: 617-934-2427
www.bibliomotion.com

Printed in the United States of America

Library of Congress Cataloging-in-Publication Data

Brown, Paul B.
  Entrepreneurship for the rest of us : how to create innovation and opportunity everywhere / Paul B. Brown.
      pages cm
  Summary: "Entrepreneurship for the Rest of Us reveals the best practices of the most successful entrepreneurs, those who are adept at continually innovating and seeing opportunity where others do not" — Provided by publisher.
  ISBN 978-1-62956-055-7 (hardback) — ISBN 978-1-62956-056-4 (ebook) — ISBN 978-1-62956-057-1 (enhanced ebook)
  1. Entrepreneurship.   2. Creative ability in business.   3. Success in business.
4. Employee motivation.   I. Title.
  HB615.B763 2015
  658.4'21—dc23
                    2014040276

For Ali,
I think it is pretty clear by now
I wouldn't last four minutes without you.

CONTENTS

CHAPTER 1

How This Book Can Help You

Great entrepreneurs don't write great books. In fact, they don't write many books at all. Neither fact is surprising. Successful entrepreneurs are typically too busy innovating to write down much of anything. And on those rare occasions when they attempt to create a book, it is filled with what they did and not with what led to their innovative idea in the first place. As a rule, accomplished entrepreneurs are not particularly introspective.

So if we want to know what makes entrepreneurs successful—in order to improve our own companies, whether we work for a huge corporation or our own start-up, or even if we are just thinking about going out on our own—we need to study them. And that is exactly what I have been doing for the last thirty years, first as the editor at *Forbes* in charge of the magazine's Up-and-Comer section, then as creator of the *New York Times* online column devoted to the skills and tools entrepreneurs need, and now as a consultant who works with small and growing companies, authors books on entrepreneurship, and writes about the topic for *Inc.* magazine, both the print and online versions.

In short, you are about to read what I have learned about

entrepreneurs over the last three decades distilled into a series of lessons and "how-tos" that can benefit both individuals and leaders at all companies, especially—and perhaps surprisingly—the world's larger ones.

That is no small point. It is virtually impossible today to read about a large company without seeing comments from the CEO, saying, "We need to be more innovative and create more products and services faster." Given their size, large companies struggle with both those objectives. They have streamlined what they could, and partnered where they can, and still they have a hard time being innovative. They are looking for help, and it simply makes sense for them to learn how the companies that are best at innovation—the nation's most successful entrepreneurial companies—handle the challenge. And they will find those lessons here.

> If we want to learn how to be more creative and more agile, it makes sense to study those who do those things best: serial entrepreneurs—people who have started two or more successful companies.

As the book's title promises, this really *is* entrepreneurship for the rest of us, a guide to creating innovation and opportunity everywhere. Consider this to be the *In Search of Excellence for Small Companies.*

And just as *In Search of Excellence*—coauthored by my friend Tom Peters (he wrote the foreword for *Customers for Life,* the book I did with Carl Sewell)—showed many executives that they were thinking about management in the wrong way, when people working at large companies look at how the best entrepreneurs actually do things, they will understand that they (perhaps like you) have been thinking about entrepreneurs and entrepreneurship all wrong.

What the Best Entrepreneurs Have in Common

I was as guilty as anyone when it came to thinking about entrepreneurs. Standard reporting (mine included, I am afraid) tends to focus on what entrepreneurs do: how they built their companies; how they handle marketing; their approach to financing their business. And if you take that approach—as just about everyone does—you would conclude that there isn't much to be gained by studying them. Each entrepreneur's behavior is as idiosyncratic as she is.

But we are not going to spend a lot of time looking at entrepreneurs' behavior in the pages ahead. We are going to study how the most successful entrepreneurs think. And if you do that, you find remarkable similarities in the way they go about creating their companies. They:

1. Figure out what they really want to do, they get a firm handle on what they want to create.
2. Take a small step toward that goal.
3. Pause after taking that small step to see what they have learned.
4. Build off that learning and take another small step.
5. Pause after taking that step.
6. Build off what they learned from taking that second step and take another small step...

If we were to reduce their process to a formula, it would be: Act, Learn, Build, Repeat. In other words, successful entrepreneurs don't spend a lot of time planning or playing "what if" games. They start (with a small step) and see how the world responds.

That just makes sense. You never truly know how the universe is going to react until you give it something to react to. So, in the face of an unknown future, entrepreneurs act. There are three wonderful benefits if you follow their lead:

3

- You can get started right away.
- You don't need a lot of resources.
- You can respond quickly to market needs.

As we will see, the best entrepreneurs deal with uncertainty not by trying to analyze it or preparing for every contingency or predicting what the outcomes will be. Instead, they act, learn from what they find, and then—based on that learning—act again. This framework becomes our starting point—and not surprisingly also makes up the content of chapter 2, "How Entrepreneurs Think," where we go into the process in much more detail.

As long as we have begun talking about the way the book is going to lay out, let's briefly discuss the whole thing so you can see how you can benefit. Chapter 3, "Always Start with a Market Need (And Not the Great Idea)," explores a concept that is counterintuitive. Ideas are easy—I bet you can come up with ten new product or service ideas in five minutes right now. And because new ideas are plentiful, they are not worth very much. As with anything else, if there is a glut—of ideas, in this case—the price goes down.

Besides, there is no guarantee anyone will buy the great idea you have come up with. The folks who created Iridium serve as a case in point. The Iridium phone was a truly wonderful invention. I am guessing here, but I am willing to bet that the inspiration for the product was this: "Wouldn't it be great if we created a cell phone that allowed you to call or e-mail anyone in the world from anywhere in the world at any time? And when I say anywhere, I mean *anywhere*. You are standing at the North Pole and want to call your spouse in Melbourne, Australia? No problem. You are on vacation in the middle of the Pacific Ocean and want to check in with your New York office? A piece of cake. You're flying on a plane thirty-five thousand feet above Moscow and need to reach someone in Cleveland? Done. Who wouldn't want a phone capable of delivering communications to and from the most remote areas in the world, where absolutely no other form of communication is available?"

When you ask the question that way, the answer would be: of course everyone is going to want one. But when you started giving people a bit more information ("The phones are going to cost what?!" And "How much a month?!" Plus "The charge per minute is going to be WHAT??!!), you would quickly realize that the number of people who want the phone *and are willing to pay for it* is not large enough to support the investment.

It was a great idea. However, it is not one that is economically viable. That's why you always want to start with what the market wants. If you begin with an idea, you need to go searching for customers who may or may not be there. If you start with the market need, the customers are assured. They are the people who have told you they need the product or service.

The takeaway: if you can discover a market need—and can fill it in a way customers like—you can make a fortune. But intriguingly, that is not the primary motivation of the people who are creating the most innovative products and services, as we will see throughout. If you look back at the early days of their companies, you will invariably find that the best entrepreneurs don't have making a fortune on their list of objectives. (It just was an extremely pleasant by-product.)

Why didn't they set off to become rich? Well, if your primary objective is to get rich quick, or to increase your organization's profits dramatically virtually overnight, you are bound to cut corners, shortchange your customers, and fail to take the time to truly understand what the market needs. You'll focus on today's sale and not the importance of building a long-term relationship with your customers. And that is true whether you are trying to get your company off the ground or are working for a large company that is introducing a new product or service in order to make this quarter's numbers.

As we will see in chapter 3, if you don't understand what the market wants, you are making your life far harder than it has to be. So instead of seeking riches, the best entrepreneurs decide that they are going to focus on an area where they feel strong and where there appears to be a market need. That's where they start to build their companies. They focus on trying to give the market what it wants (chapter 3) and conclude—correctly as we will see—that if they do that well, by competing differently (chapter 4) their business will succeed. How do they market? The conventional wisdom— find a niche, zig when others zag—is right, but not particularly helpful for either potential start-ups or established companies. It lacks, to be kind, specificity. It's far better to describe what the best entrepreneurs do, and that is "compete differently." And that's what we will be talking about in chapter 4. We'll see how the best entrepreneurs:

- **Make small bets**
- **Make those small bets quickly**
- **Build off an existing idea**
- **Let the market define their product or service**
- **Take one step at a time**

That is what they do instead of setting out to be rich (chapter 5). This bring us to perhaps the biggest area that people fail to understand—financing, the subject of chapter 6. With all the attention paid to venture capitalists, there is a mistaken impression that the best entrepreneurs begin their companies with millions of dollars in start-up financing. That simply isn't true. The average cost, as we are going to see, is slightly more than $100,000, and that figure includes the (relatively few) companies, such as biotech firms, that need millions to begin.

Sure, that number isn't chicken feed, but the figure is not particularly daunting. Why is it so low, relatively speaking? As chapter 6 explains, it's low because of the way the best entrepreneurs launch their companies. They are taking small steps, so they only need sufficient financing to accomplish the next one. (And, obviously, proceeding this way makes it easier for larger companies to try more and different ideas, since the risk is relatively small.)

Once entrepreneurs know the fundamentals of creating their business—or leaders in large organizations understand their entrepreneurial objective—they need to determine how they are going to go about it. That brings us to chapter 7, "Building the Team."

The company founder needs to delegate early. As the founder, you can try to micromanage, but it is ultimately self-defeating because you stifle growth—your organization can never get larger than what you can handle effectively. You need to get others involved from day one.

But the biggest surprise, when it comes to people, is that the best entrepreneurs find a yin to their yang. They find people who offset their weakness and complement their strengths.

> Walt Disney had Roy Disney, Steve Jobs had Steve Wozniak, and Orville Wright had Wilbur Wright. Wherever there is great innovation, there is both a dreamer and an operator, an "idea" person and one who turns those ideas into reality. It is rare for one person to have both those skills.

The biggest lesson in this chapter?

1. Determine where your passions lie.
2. Find an equally passionate (complementary) partner.
3. Go change the world.

Speaking of changing the world, chapter 8 is titled "How the Most Successful Entrepreneurs Turn Obstacles into Assets." I am not big on clichés like "Every time God closes a door He opens a window" or "There are no problems, only opportunities," but the best entrepreneurs believe and act as if everything is a gift. Well, maybe not every single thing imaginable. But assuming that every experience is a gift is a good way of looking at the problems and surprises you'll encounter in any endeavor, such as getting a new venture off the ground, obtaining buy-in from your boss, or launching a new product line in an ultracompetitive market.

Why take this seemingly Pollyannaish approach? There are three key reasons. First, you are going to find out eventually what people do and do not like about your idea. It's better to learn these things as soon as possible, before you sink more resources into the concept, venture, or product line. You always want to keep potential losses to a minimum so that you can live to fight another day.

Second, the feedback could take you in another direction or help you set up a barrier to competition. You thought you wanted to start a public relations firm but a quick survey told you potential customers thought the field was saturated. However, more than a few of the people you talked with said they would love someone who could help with their *internal* communications.

Third, you get evidence. True, it may not have been what you expected or hoped for, but the evidence you collected still puts you ahead of the person who is just thinking about doing something (like opening another PR firm). You know something he doesn't, and that is an asset. You are ahead of the game.

But what if it's really bad news? It's a disappointment. You were absolutely certain that your boss would approve your idea for a new software program, and she said no in a way that is still echoing down the corridor. No reasonable person can define what you've encountered as anything but a problem, and most people will try to solve the problem. ("Maybe she will like the idea if I go at it this way instead.") That's fine, if you can find a workable solution. If you do, the problem has gone away and, again, you've learned something that others might not know (the boss hates Y, but she loves Z).

But what if you can't solve the "problem" (she hated Z, too)? Accept the situation to the point of embracing it. Take as a given that it won't ever change, and turn the difficulty into an asset. What can you do with this fact? Maybe the problem presents a heretofore unseen opportunity. Maybe you build it into your product or service in a way that no competitor (having not acted) could imagine. Could you take the resolved problem and do something with it on your own? Could you take the new idea to a competitor and use it as your calling card to look for the next job?

The thing to remember is this: successful people work with what they have at hand—whatever comes along—and try to use everything at their disposal to achieve their goals. And that is why they are grateful for surprises, obstacles, and even disappointments. It gives them more information and resources to draw upon.

The final chapter takes us full circle. We'll explore, in depth, how entrepreneurs motivate themselves (and stay motivated) for the long haul.

If chapter 9 is the final chapter, why have an afterword? Well, I wanted to talk directly to people who are on the fence about taking the entrepreneurial plunge; after all, some of the people reading this book don't (yet) have companies of their own. The afterword's title addresses the biggest concern they have: "Being an Entrepreneur Is Less Scary Than You Think." And here's why I included it. Although it may seem like a distant memory, it really wasn't all that long ago that working for a large company was the safest thing in the world. You traded a reasonable day's work for a reasonable paycheck and lived happily after. Well, that was then, and endless "rightsizings" and layoffs are now. Today, you'd be hard pressed to find anyone who hasn't thought about going out on her own.

If the perceived risk is one of the reasons you are holding back, you'll read here that striking out on your own may not be as frightening as you think. That's according to the people who deal best with an unknown future, the country's most accomplished entrepreneurs. There's a reason seasoned entrepreneurs don't think of themselves as risk takers, even though everyone else does. They have developed terrific ways to limit potential losses as they start new ventures.

Yes, of course, the cliché is that entrepreneurs leap before looking and bet everything on one roll of the dice. But in reality that isn't true. The best entrepreneurs adhere to the basic principles of risk management. That means that if you're going to play in a game with uncertain outcomes, you never:

1. Pay/bet more than what you can expect as a return.
2. Pay/bet more than you can afford to lose.

Both these ideas can be summed up with the phrase "acceptable loss," which means that you consider the potential downside of whatever risk you are about to take—starting a new company or a venture that is going to consume a lot of your time, capital, or other assets—and put on the line no more than you find it tolerable to lose should the venture not turn out the way you want.

What has worked for these other entrepreneurs will work for you, providing you understand this is *not* how we were taught to think about risk. In the predictable world we were all trained in, you'd spend a *lot* of time estimating the size of the prize—the potential financial rewards associated with a particular opportunity—and optimizing the plan to achieve what those in the finance community call "the expected return." The logic of this approach is straightforward and looks something like this:

1. Analyze the prospective market and choose segments with the highest potential return.
2. Develop and optimize the plan for your product or service to achieve that return.
3. Calculate the costs in money, time, and resources of achieving your goal.

If you work at a big company, this should sound very familiar. It's a result of years of conditioning designed to "maximize shareholder wealth." But while this logic makes enormous sense in a predictable setting, it is just silly in the face of an unknown, as when you are introducing a new product or service. If you follow those steps for unpredictable events, however, all you end up doing is making projections...based on assumptions...that are contingent on guesses...which are based on....Finally, you pretend that you are creating certainty by multiplying the whole thing by something less than 100 percent, to compensate for uncertainty and so that you appear to be making rational decisions. But the more uncertain the situation—and, as a glance at the daily newspapers shows, the universe seems to get more unpredictable by the moment—the more foolish this math is.

And that explains why entrepreneurs and other creators use a different logic, that of acceptable loss. Instead of focusing on expected return—or how much they could possibly make—their attention is on acceptable loss—how much they are willing to lose should things not turn out the way they hope.

Employing the concept of acceptable loss keeps any failures small. By definition, you never lose more than you are willing to. If you fail, you fail cheaply and quickly, and that is far better than investing a lot of time, money, and other resources only to see the project not work out.

With all this by way of background, let's look at the principles in detail.

CHAPTER 2

How the Best Entrepreneurs Think

We will get into the nuts and bolts of how entrepreneurs think in a minute, but let's begin with a story that you might have read in a business magazine a couple of years back.

Salsa Queen

Hard work, relentless determination, and the willingness to go it alone has allowed H. Harriet Harrison to carve out a new niche in one of the fastest-growing food markets—and has made her extremely rich in the process.

By Charles M. Wilheim

Before answering, H. (for Hillary) Harriet Harrison stole a quick look at the framed stock certificate hanging on the wall of her office just outside Bozeman, Montana.

"It *is* amazing, isn't it," she said. "For three years—1,058 days, to be exact, I kept track—I lived on nothing but store-brand pasta with ketchup, salad, and apples, and now..." she gestured out the window at her 400-acre horse ranch, the first thing she bought with some of the $90 million she received from selling 59% of her company, Yummy Olé: The American Salsa Co., in a public offering the month before.

Harrison, as entrepreneur-founders often do, had stood on the floor of the New York Stock Exchange (NYSE) and bought the first 100 shares of her initial public offering (IPO). It was those shares—now in an ornate gold frame with a tiny spotlight beaming down on it—that she kept glancing at every 20 seconds. It was as if she needed to constantly make sure she wasn't dreaming that she was suddenly worth almost $600 million (the money she received from the IPO, coupled with the value of her remaining 41% of the company), and that those thousand-plus arduous days were behind her.

"And those three years don't even include the six months I spent searching for the right idea," she added.

Harrison, now 34, was a brand manager at Kraft who had been itching to go out on her own, but she could never find a business concept that resonated with her.

"Finally, I said, 'To hell with financial security.' I quit Kraft and promised myself I would find the perfect idea for a company. I thought it would take me about a week."

Inspiration struck on day 174.

"I had been poring through analyst reports, talking to everyone I knew, constantly visiting supermarkets and restaurants, and reading all the trade publications. The thing that kept jumping out at me was that salsa had replaced ketchup as the best-selling condiment in America. Salsa—you should excuse the pun—was hot. I knew there was an opportunity there. But I couldn't figure out what it was. I spent months beating my head against the wall, trying to figure out how I could get a piece of the market.

"I was so frustrated that one morning I called up a girl-friend and asked her to meet me for lunch, just so I could get away for a while. And it was while I was at a TGI Fridays, of all places, that the lightbulb finally went on over my head."

And a Little Child Shall Lead Her

"While I was waiting for Claire, I looked over at the next table. A young couple was trying to convince their toddler, strapped into a high chair, to eat something. He just wouldn't. I figured he didn't like the taste or texture of what they were offering.

"I didn't think much of it. I continued to look around the restaurant and skimmed another analyst report. For some reason, when I looked back at the table with the toddler, I glanced at what the father was having for lunch, and I saw he had small dish of salsa, not ketchup, to put on his burger. That's when it all came together.

"Yes, salsa is popular. But there had to be some portion of the market that, like the baby, didn't like the taste or texture. I thought, 'If you could make salsa more ketchup-like, you'd have a winner.'

"I went home, looked up every salsa recipe I could find, and started working on ways to smooth out the texture and make the product a bit sweeter. It sounds simple, right? But I had to isolate every variable. Fresh tomatoes or canned? Regular sugar, natural sweeteners, or a sugar substitute? Could you go with fresh tomatoes and cooked vegetables? Must every vegetable be fresh?

"It turns out there were six key variables, and I tested every combination. That means I tried 720 different recipes. Even creating two of them a day, every day—weekends, holidays, no matter what—took me a full year.

"My friends kept telling me to let it go. Good enough would be good enough, and I could always refine things later. Or they suggested I simply sell my recipe to a solid company like Kraft and take a tiny royalty on every jar sold. And there were a bunch of folks I know who suggested I partner with someone like Heinz, which had the distribution and marketing in place. But all those things struck me as wrong. My name was going to be behind the product. I had to be the one who was satisfied. So, I continued creating two recipes a day, trying to find the right one. I wasn't going to go out into the marketplace until it was perfect."

When she finally got the recipe right, Harrison starting driving throughout the Helena area, where she was living at the time, trying to get supermarkets and restaurants to buy a jar or two.

"God, it was hard. I'd make six, seven, eight sales calls a day, and get one sale every two days. Then I'd go home depressed, make myself some pasta because it was quick and cheap, and then I'd create another batch of salsa and do it again the next day."

Eventually, she started making a sale a day, then two and three a day. Most of the people who bought her product loved it and reordered. Within six months she had hired a couple of part-time cooks to whip up the salsa, and within a year she was subcontracting to a food manufacturer and hiring a national sales firm.

Still, "It wasn't until year three that I was actually able to take a salary. I know it sounds like a cliché, but I really did max out my credit cards, taking cash advances from one to pay another, and as the bills came due I borrowed from anyone I could (thanks, Mom and Dad).

"I remember the day exactly; it was June 16, a Thursday, when I thought I could afford to have something other than pasta for dinner. That was day 1,059 since I had started the company. I made myself tuna salad and had two glasses from a $4 bottle of wine I was saving for just that occasion."

A year later, underwriters at Kidder, Peabody would be buying her lobster and champagne in New York as they tried to convince her (successfully, as it turned out) to let them take her company public. Eleven months later, Harrison was standing on the floor of the NYSE buying those 100 shares of Yummy Olé: The *American* Salsa Co. (ticker symbol: YOUS [pronounced "Yo, U.S." by traders]).

"And now here you are, writing about my overnight success," Harrison says with a laugh. "Is there any advice I'd offer? Not really. I think my journey is pretty typical. But if I were forced to say something, I'd say stick to your guns and remain true to your vision—the salsa we sell today uses exactly the same recipe I came up with initially. Remain passionate about your idea at all times, and keep plugging."

You probably found this article familiar. But it didn't appear in *Inc.*, the late *Fortune Small Business*, or the small business section of the *Wall Street Journal*. And you won't find it in the archives of *Success*, *Entrepreneur*, the Up-and-Comers column of *Forbes*, nor, for that matter, in any other publication—online or print—that devotes space on a regular basis to the doings of entrepreneurs.

I made up every bit of it.

And I did so for two reasons. First, I think it captures the slightly reverent tone the press takes in writing about successful entrepreneurs. It is as if they are describing a magic trick that they don't understand, and so they have trouble being properly skeptical.

Second, and far more important, just about every trait attributed to H. (for Hillary) Harriet Harrison embodies the conventional wisdom about how entrepreneurs act. And just about all of that conventional wisdom is wrong. I wanted to expose these myths for two interrelated reasons:

• By picturing entrepreneurs as a unique heroic species, we end up believing that there are only a handful of people who can become successful entrepreneurs and that they succeed because they are hardwired at birth to start their own companies. Nothing could be further from the truth. Not only can everyone employ the same approach to solving problems that entrepreneurs use, entrepreneurs' reasoning can be learned.

• As you will see, the methods that entrepreneurs employ as they go about creating something new draws on a form of reasoning that we were all born with. It is drummed out of us as we go through school. (In the pages ahead, I will show you how to regain that skill.)

But before we get into all that, we need to address the myths surrounding entrepreneurs and entrepreneurship for one simple reason. If we are to create innovation and opportunity everywhere— whether we work for a large organization or a start-up—we need to know how the best people do it. That way, we can build on their approach instead of having to create everything ourselves. We need to wipe away the myths so that we can understand how the best entrepreneurs think.

It Ain't Necessarily So

The easiest way to talk about the myths surrounding entrepreneurs is to go back to the story of the imaginary Salsa Queen. I'll state the myth, show how Harrison embodied that fiction, and then describe what typically happens instead. The myths tend to fall into three big categories.

Myth #1: Entrepreneurs Concentrate on One Perfect Idea

Harriet spent "six months...searching for the right idea." The reality is that entrepreneurs—just like the rest of us—can come up with a dozen potentially commercial ideas before breakfast, if they set their minds to it.

The problem isn't coming up with an idea. It is figuring out which one you want to spend your time on. (We will talk in detail about that decision in chapter 3, but to foreshadow the argument: it is always easier to start by solving a market need than to come up with a radically new idea.)

Related to the myth of the "perfect" idea is the belief that an idea comes into an entrepreneur's head fully formed. Remember when Harriet said she glanced at the salsa on the dad's plate, and then back to the baby, and "that's when it all came together"—she knew the world wanted a smoother, sweeter salsa?

I concede that this occurs every once in a while, just like love at first sight actually happens sometimes and there are some people who know at the age of three that they were born to be doctors and then actually become physicians. But the reality is that, in the majority of cases, the potential entrepreneur has a vague notion along the lines of "Hmm, I have all these skills"—in marketing, in Harriet's case—"and I wonder what I can do with them?" or "I know all these people (or I can access these kinds of specific resources) and I wonder how I can use them to create a product or service that people want?"

The last part of the myth we have to bust involves the belief that once the idea is fully formed, it is sacred. Even though Harriet developed *the perfect sweet salsa formula* and said that it never changed ("The salsa we sell today uses exactly the same recipe I came up with up initially"), she actually followed the serial entrepreneur's recipe of always tweaking his ideas. Remember, Harriet went through 720 variations. Most people don't do that many. But just about every successful entrepreneur changes his product and/or business model, sometimes dramatically, as he gets underway.

Initially Howard Schultz, who built the Starbucks chain, had Italian opera playing as background music at his coffee shops. Michael Dell began his company by doing nothing more than assembling IBM personal computer knockoffs. The best entrepreneurs don't wait to see if their product or service is perfect before they start searching to see if the market will accept it. They get out into the marketplace with something close to what they want to sell, see how potential customers react, and adjust the product accordingly.

Entrepreneurs are flexible when it comes to advertising and selling too. Their marketing plans are not locked in stone, as the entrepreneurial myths would have you believe. As you'll remember, during the start-up phase of Yummy Olé, people suggested to Harriet that she "simply sell [her] recipe to a solid company like Kraft and take a tiny royalty on every jar sold. And there were a bunch of folks...who suggested partnering with someone like Heinz, which had the distribution and marketing in place."

Harriet ignored those ideas because she was convinced that she *knew* how to build her brand. The best entrepreneurs, however, are open to advice. They seek it out. They don't always take it, but they don't reject out of hand something that could help them. They would have explored whether selling or partnering early on would have made sense. Maybe they would have sold the recipe or partnered with an established company. Maybe they wouldn't have. But they would have explored such an arrangement rather than dismissing it out of hand.

Myth #2: It Is the Lone Genius Who Creates the New

As you will recall, Harriet tried hundreds of separate recipes in her kitchen, experimenting until she was happy. And this is perhaps the most pervasive myth of all: the entrepreneur comes up with the idea alone. Not true. Even the most celebrated inventors (like Thomas Alva Edison) worked in conjunction with others. Harriet had no employees, and certainly no partners, during the early days. She cooked the salsa at night and went out and tried to sell it the next day. In reality, successful serial entrepreneurs often involve other people from the very beginning, believing that "All of us together are smarter than any one of us."

And because they work with others, they don't necessarily spend twenty-four hours a day every day, as Harriet did, developing their idea. Remember, long before she was cooking by night and selling by day, she was trying out recipes. "Even creating two of them a day, every day—weekends, holidays, no matter what—took me a full year." While it is certainly true that some entrepreneurs work constantly, the same can be said about some doctors, lawyers, plumbers, and candlestick makers. How much time someone spends on the job is a personal decision—and that is true of entrepreneurs too.

Myth #3: Entrepreneurs Commit Totally Early in the Process

You'll recall that Harriet created a burning platform for herself. ("I said, 'To hell with financial security.' I quit Kraft and promised myself I would find the perfect idea for a company.") Well, that rarely happens. Entrepreneurs are people, too. They have lives, families, and financial obligations. They don't say, "To hell with financial security" on a whim. They commit after careful thought, and even then they don't bet everything they have. (More on this in a minute.)

Harriet says she lived exclusively on pasta, salad, and apples for three years. And while she admits it is a cliché, she adds that she funded her venture using her credit cards. Again, you can find examples where this is true—especially if the entrepreneur is young and has no financial commitments (no family to support, no mortgage to pay, etc.). But in the vast majority of cases, entrepreneurs don't bet everything on one roll of the dice. Like the rest of us, they simply couldn't take that big a chance. You never want to bet the house, because you are always going to need someplace to live.

Moving on

What are we left with, after we have addressed all these myths? Just this: entrepreneurs, like the rest of us, prefer to think their journey is unique and, also like the rest of us, they sometimes remember their past in ways that are more heroic than accurate. But, really, they are not especially different from you or me. They are not more heroic. They don't have x-ray vision that allows them to spot holes in the marketplace, and they don't have a special gene that allows them to succeed.

So what makes entrepreneurs entrepreneurs? There are two overwhelming traits that jump out from the research, and these can be combined and summarized in twelve words: **Entrepreneurs have a passion for discovering opportunities. Once they do, they act.**

Part of that statement is self-evident, of course. Entrepreneurs do. They act. If you just sit around and think of ideas for new products or services, but don't *do* anything with those thoughts, you are not an entrepreneur. You are just someone with a lot of unrealized ideas. But it is how entrepreneurs act that is most important. So let's examine that part of the process in detail.

How the Best Entrepreneurs Do Things

What can get lost in the fictional story of H. Harriet Harrison is the part that is almost universally true. She *wanted* to start a company of her own. That desire cannot—and should not—be underestimated, although it almost always is.

Desire is what gets people from just thinking about an idea to actually making it happen. It's what's keeps people going in the face of the inevitable obstacles that come along. And it is what attracts others to the enterprise, compelling them to join the entrepreneur's journey. It is a powerful force indeed.

On the surface, it seems there are four questions you might ask before starting any new venture:

1. Is it feasible? That is, is it within the realm of reality?
2. Can I do it? Is it feasible for *me*?
3. Is it worth doing? Will there be a market for what I want to sell, is there potential to turn a profit, and will people appreciate what I am trying to do? In other words, does it make sense to put in all this effort?
4. Do I want to do it?

This last question is the one that really matters: **Do you want to create it?** Either the venture is something that you want or it's something that leads to something you want. If it is neither of these, there's no reason to act or to answer the other three questions. There is simply no way you are going to give your endeavor your full effort if your heart isn't in it, at least to some degree.

Once you want to do something, everything gets reframed. The negative emotional response to all the unknowns is reduced. The reality hasn't changed: you still don't know what is out there. But you'll find a way around the problem because you care about what you are trying to do. That is why the desire is so important.

Okay, the desire is in place, what do you do now? Most people think they need to do a lot of research to get confirmation that they are on to something and to fine-tune what they have. Well, they are right about the second part of that sentence. You want confirmation and you want to tailor your offering to market needs.

But you don't need to do months (or years) of research or planning. Heck, you don't even need a finished prototype. Tell people about your idea, show them a sketch, or, in the case of a food product, let them taste a sample.

> Much of the conventional wisdom about entrepreneurs and entrepreneurship is simply wrong.

Do the minimal amount of research, just enough to convince yourself the idea is a good one, and then get out into the marketplace and ask people to give you an order. If the answer is yes, you have done all the research you need.

So, we have just defined the next thing to do, after you determine your desire: you take a small step toward your goal and see what happens. You go to a representative sample of your potential market, and say, "I am thinking of opening an Italian restaurant at Fourth and Main. What do you think?" There is no huge outlay of capital in doing that. There are no leases to sign. No equipment to buy. You simply ask a group of restaurant-goers (in this case) whether your idea makes sense.

The next step? You learn from the last one. What did your potential market say? In the case of the potential restaurant, there really are only three possible responses:

1. What a great idea.
2. Maybe I'd eat there.
3. No, I would probably never give you a try.

You'd learn from each response. Let's begin with "no." You want to find out why someone rejected the idea. It could be that there are already a lot of Italian restaurants—at various price points—in the area, and potential customers have no interest in trying a new one because they already have their favorite(s). At this point, many potential entrepreneurs make a critical mistake. They say, "Ah, but people haven't seen *my* vision. Once they do, they will be beating the doors down to get in." That almost never happens. Going ahead with the precise idea that people have told you they do not want is the fastest way I know to lose a fortune. But perhaps those restaurant-goers say, as they reject your idea, "You know, there really isn't a place around here to get a good steak." That response could take you in a different direction.

If you get a "yes" or a "maybe" when you ask about opening an Italian restaurant, you then take another small step toward your goal. You might ask, for example, should we be open for both lunch and dinner or only dinner? And you keep asking questions—and evaluating the answers—until you are convinced you are on to something or that it is time to find another idea.

The process I just described is exactly how the best entrepreneurs build their companies, all the stories about the H. Harriet Harrisons of the world to the contrary. The best entrepreneurs:

- Figure out what they want.
- Take a small step toward their goal.
- Pause after taking that small step to see what they learned.
- Build that learning into their next step.
- Pause after taking that step, etc.

We can reduce this to shorthand: Act. Learn. Build. Repeat. It is a model that companies from Alibaba to Facebook to Starbucks have followed.

Let's see how the salsa story would have played out if our fictional entrepreneur had followed the real path that most successful entrepreneurs take. For one thing, H. Harriet Harrison probably would not have quit her day job so early. Odds are, she would have been searching for an idea on nights, weekends, and her lunch hour. Entrepreneurs, like the rest of us, have bills to pay and families to take care of. They don't quit their jobs on a whim.

But even after she had found an idea, she still would not have quit. Remember, the best entrepreneurs take small steps toward their goal. Quitting your day job is a big one. Odds are, Harriet would have first asked a representative sample of people if the idea of a more ketchup-like salsa was appealing. If the response was promising, she would have whipped up a few batches.

If she were operating as successful entrepreneurs do, Harriet would not have made herself the final arbiter of what the market wanted. She would have had people sample various test recipes— probably no more than five (remember, we are trying to get underway quickly)—and then started selling her homemade salsas at craft fairs and farmers' markets to gain traction and to make sure she didn't go too deeply into debt.

As she sold the product, she would get feedback. What did people like? The fact that it was not too spicy? What did they not like? Perhaps they wanted the consistency to be more like ketchup than salsa?

She would let the market constantly define the product, even after she got it into stores. The formula would not be locked in place, although if she (and the market) truly liked a recipe she would probably keep it and then come up with additional variations— salsa with a hint of mango, sweet salsa, lime-flavored salsa—and offer them as line extensions. You always want to expand your market when you can.

This Act-Learn-Build-Repeat model may not be as sexy as the fictional story of Ms. Harrison's salsa company, but it really is the way the best entrepreneurs go about building their companies. And it is the most efficient way to go.

Takeaways for Entrepreneurs and the Rest of Us

1. Don't reinvent the proverbial wheel. You don't need to learn everything the hard way. Serial entrepreneurs—people who have created two or more successful companies—have a proven approach to creating innovation and opportunity. The approach that has worked for them will work for you.

2. Despite the myths, the best entrepreneurs take small steps—not giant leaps—as they go about creating something new; they work with others and are extremely receptive to feedback and suggestions.

3. The formula the best entrepreneurs follow is: Act. Learn. Build. Repeat. This approach works for individuals, start-ups, and large organizations that want to innovate and create opportunity. You should use it, too.

CHAPTER 3

Always Start with a Market Need (And Not the Great Idea)

I have a thought."

"What about...?"

"This is so crazy, it might work. Why don't we..."

"I've got it!"

You can find endless variations on the "eureka" moment in books, television, movies, and media of all types. You know the scene: the proverbial light goes on over someone's head and he comes up with the idea that saves the day. This moment is a staple in storytelling of all kinds—fiction and non—and probably has been since cave dwellers took charred sticks and started drawing pictures on the walls of their homes. Invariably, the pivotal (and correct) idea comes at just the right moment to save the day (win the girl, repel the invaders, be awarded the account, save the farm...).

Coming up with the right idea at just the right time is certainly dramatic. But is *the right idea* the place where the best entrepreneurs start their search for a winning business?

No.

And all those fictional scenes from movies, TV, and the like contain the seeds of the explanation. Think about where the "I got an idea" scene always occurs. It happens at the moment when everything hinges on the idea being right. If it isn't, bad things are going to happen. It is a great dramatic plot point.

However, in real life—as opposed to reel life—there is absolutely no guarantee the idea is going to work, and who wants to wait until the very last second only to discover that they bet on the wrong horse. There is no way to recover should that happen. Failure at that point is fatal.

But the difficulty with betting everything on the idea starts long before that pivotal moment. The first problem with starting with the idea is that it is too easy. I'd wager you could come up with ideas for twenty-five new businesses in the next half hour if you sat down and made a list. But how would you ever know if they had commercial appeal? If your idea does not make money—or make the world a substantially better place, if you are starting a nonprofit—it is not a viable idea. It's just a whim. Something to do to pass the time.

Sure, you concede that commuting to work by giant pogo stick might be financially viable, but some of your ideas—like your desire to create a tomato-flavored soda—could have potential. After all, there have to be millions of people like you who *love* tomatoes and can't get enough. (Don't dismiss that tomato soda idea out of hand. If the soft drink brand Dr. Brown's can successfully sell its Cel-Ray soda—which does indeed sort of taste like celery—then maybe there is a shot for a tomato-based soda.)

The tomato-y soft drink example does, however, underscore another problem with beginning with the idea: often, people create something designed to fill a particular need they have or eliminate a specific problem that has been vexing them. Can that approach work? Sure. Healthy Choice frozen meals were created, according to ConAgra, because its CEO had suffered a heart attack and was looking for good-tasting foods he could eat as part of restricted diet and prepare by himself in a hurry.

But, just because you desire something doesn't mean there are enough people like you to make it a viable product. Let's take me as an example. I like to cook. And I love English murder mysteries. And I can't be the only person in the universe who falls into both those categories. So, why not create a line of cookware—pots, pans, skillets, and so on—inspired by Sherlock Holmes? The Holmes character has been popular for more than 125 years, and is always being rediscovered by the television and movie industries, so why not take advantage of that fact?

The idea would either work or it wouldn't—and since I am not going to be doing anything with it, feel free to steal it—but it shows you another problem with beginning with the idea. Once you come up with an idea like Sherlock Holmes cookware, you have to search for a market. How would you go about finding people like me? I don't read cooking magazines, watch cooking shows, or go to mystery conventions, and I am not a member of the Mystery of the Month Club. That search could be time consuming and expensive. Even worse, it could be ultimately fruitless, depending on how you go about it.

Remember the Iridium phone we talked about in chapter 1? It would have been exactly the sort of thing I would have invented (if I had a taken a science course after eleventh grade and had any technological aptitude). The idea that you could call from literally anywhere in the world to anywhere was simply wonderful.

And it bombed. Not because of the technology—that worked great—but because of how much its maker had to charge.

The Iridium story, and everything else we have talked about up until now, explains why starting with an idea is not the approach that the best entrepreneurs take. Like them, you want to begin by solving an existing need.

There are three specific reasons for that. One, you won't have to spend a lot of time explaining what you have. Photochromic lenses—eyeglass lenses that automatically darken to become sunglass when you are outside and become clear again when you go back indoors—serve as a case in point. They were eventually a success, but it took decades. People knew what glasses were. And they knew what sunglasses were. But glasses that turned into sunglasses and back again? That had them confused. It took a lot of explaining and demonstrating. Consumers needed to understand what the product was and then they had to be convinced it actually worked. If people have a need, there isn't a lot of explaining to do. Your pitch? "You have a need for a product/service that does X? Here it is."

For another thing, you have a ready-made market. You are creating a product or service for people who have told you they need it. There is not a whole lot of time wasted looking for customers.

And finally, you can move substantially faster. The scope of what you are trying to do is remarkably clear. You are trying to solve a specific need. Everything else is irrelevant. You focus on filling the need and only the need.

Drilling Down a Bit Deeper

While just about every successful entrepreneur agrees with the idea that you want to start with a market need and not an idea, they break into two camps over just how to go about discovering that need.

Do you find an unexpressed need, à la Apple, creating wonderful products that people do not know they need until they see it (things like the iPod or MacBook Air), or do you simply take an existing idea and improve upon it (the build-a-better-mousetrap approach)?

Either path has a lot to recommend it. G. Michael Maddock—who founded and runs the innovation consulting firm Maddock Douglas, which has helped 25 percent of the Fortune 100 create billions of dollars' worth of new products and services—is big on the idea of finding unexpressed needs. "The place to start the innovation process is by coming up with an insight into a huge problem that is waiting to be solved," Maddock says (and has written; he is the author of several books on innovation and blogs on the topic for *Forbes*). In our conversation he told me:

> Before you can start looking for an insight, you need to know what an insight is. Here's our definition: **An insight, for the purposes of innovation, must be a penetrating customer truth rich enough to generate significant ideas that can help build your business.** It must be penetrating in that it needs to be true for a large group of people. If it is not true for a lot of your target market, then your potential business opportunity is limited. In other words, if you cannot drive business with it, it's not an insight; it's interesting trivia. This is the big leagues. Interesting trivia won't allow you to build a thriving company. If that's all you have, you need to try again.

Ultimately, an insight seeks to make someone's life simpler, more convenient, more economical, or even more worthwhile.

How do you know when you're on to something? Maddock points to three factors:

1. You can express the insight in terms of a statement of fact from the customer's point of view.
2. There are clear reasons why the facts are true.
3. There is a problem, or tension, in the marketplace that needs resolution before you can give people what they want.

According to Maddock:

> If there is nothing to solve for, you may have found some-thing that is true but it is not an insight in our world. For example, "I like to eat fast food because I can get in and out of the restaurant quickly" is clearly a statement that satis-fies the first two conditions. There is a statement of fact ("I like to eat fast food") and we know why the fact is true ("because I can get out of the restaurant quickly"). But there is no tension. There is nothing to solve for. Fast food restau-rants are abundant, and no one is really clamoring for fast food to be served even faster.
>
> The same sort of situation exists if someone tells you, "I like to fly when I have a meeting that is more than three hundred miles away. It's faster."
>
> Again, we have the statement of fact and the reason why, but no tension. Plane travel has already been invented.
>
> Conversely, having a tension does two things. First, it keeps you focused. There is clarity. You know what you are solving for, the tension. Second, it makes communicating what you have substantially easier since you know what you want to talk to the customer about.

So if you want to reduce the search for insight to a formula, it would look like this:

I (FACT) because (WHY) but (TENSION).

Maddock continues:

> You are solving for the pain. You can see the difference between "I like to eat fast food because I can get in and out of the restaurant quickly" and "I like to eat fast food,

because I can get out of the restaurant quickly, but two hours later I don't feel so well because they don't always use the best ingredients."

Similarly, there is a striking difference between: "I like to fly when I have a meeting that is more than three hundred miles away. It's faster." And "I like to fly when I have a meeting that is more than three hundred miles away because it's faster, but the security lines are incredibly frustrating."

In the latter cases, you now have something to solve for. (Better-tasting fast food, for example, or creating things for people to do while they are waiting in security lines.)

Maddock's reasoning is sound. But Leonard C. Green wonders if you need to work that hard. Green, trained as an accountant, has created or been involved in fourteen businesses in fields ranging from finance and real estate to thoroughbred horses and professional sports teams so he is a man worth listening to, especially since he is a professor of entrepreneurship Babson College.

Green thinks that once you've been convinced you should start with a market need—and he believes you should—"all" you need to do is find an existing concept and improve it: "There is a reason the cliché is, build a better mousetrap, [and the world will beat a path to your door.] It is not create a better mousetrap."

The advantage of the better-mousetrap approach is threefold, Green argues. First, it is quicker to explain what you have. Once you say "better mousetrap," potential customers have a context for your creation. You are creating an improved version of an existing product. If you create something completely new, you need to spend time and money explaining to your potential customers what you have. That's the photochromatic lenses problem that we talked about earlier.

The second advantage, as Green points out, is "it allows you to move faster. You know exactly what you are trying to create—that better mousetrap."

And that bring us to the third point. It allows you to focus. Because you know you are going to be creating that better mousetrap and you can concentrate all your energies there.

So, how do you do it?

You can't simply copy what some other company is doing. You may get sued, for one thing. And for another, that doesn't give anyone a reason to buy what you have. If your product or service is the same as the original, people will go with the original. Why wouldn't they?

Green agrees, saying that is why you are making a *better* mousetrap. What makes it better? He rattles off a list of ways you can differentiate yourself from the existing product.

- **Be the low-price provider.** This is the first place people turn, typically. It is self-explanatory but, Green cautions, extremely dangerous in the long run unless you plan to become the Walmart of your industry. The problem with this approach is that a competitor—because he has found out how to do what you do, only cheaper, or really doesn't know the costs and so doesn't charge enough—can always undercut your price. It might, however, be the way to go initially, in order to get some attention and gain market share.

- **Be the high-price/high-quality provider.** You are the best in class. You can find examples everywhere you look. Blue Buffalo pet food, a company Green helped create, is at the extremely high end of the market. Other examples? Gucci, Nordstrom, and Lamborghini.

- **Have the best solution to the problem.** You offer the most reliable printer or the car that has the lowest cost to maintain.

- **Be the fastest.** Sure, car manufacturers talk about going from zero to sixty all the time—a Porsche can do it in 3.2 seconds—but that is not the only industry in which you can position around speed. You could have the fastest search engine or the fastest-growing roses.

- **Offer more convenience.** You could provide one-stop shopping, as the big-box stores (Walmart, Costco) do. "Doc-in-the-box" walk-in medical centers and companies that offer twenty-four-hour access to their order departments and customer service providers are two other examples.

- **Offer a better experience.** Going to a minor league baseball game can be more entertaining than going to a major league one, where you are cut off from the players, can't go on the field, and very little happens between innings. At a minor league game, the players are accessible and readily sign autographs, you're often allowed to run the bases after the game, and there is some sort of contest or activity between most innings and sometimes every half-inning.

   Here are two other examples Green likes. Home Depot and Lowes may seemingly stock everything, but nothing beats the local hardware store for service and advice. And older participants were finding tennis and golf too demanding, so Howard Head invented an oversized racquet and Adams Golf started selling lighter, "more forgiving" (i.e., easier-to-use) golf clubs.

- **Transport your idea.** Ideas that work in one place could very well work in another. If you think about it, this is what importing and exporting is all about. And you see the concept applied to television programming all the time. Producers take a hit show in England and bring it to the United States.

- **Combine two or more features.** Vending machines aren't new. But set them up to dispense movies and you get Redbox, the $1 video rental company. Data storage has been around for as long as there has been data. But combine it with the old-fashioned record store and you get iTunes.

Six Reasons You Don't Want to Start with an Idea

I love going to "closeout" stores. Some people call them liquidators or odd lot shops. It doesn't matter what you call them. They are the places that buy incredibly cheaply all the products (rugs, clothing, small appliances, and sporting goods) that other retailers weren't able to move—and then mark up the items slightly and offer them to you and me in a no-frills store. Invariably, the shopping carts in these stores came from department stores and supermarkets that went out of business years ago and even the bags they wrap the merchandise in carry logos of retailers that no longer exist.

As you walk through the aisles, you will find scores and scores of interesting products that simply didn't sell at what manufacturers and inventors thought was a reasonable price. Sure, some of the stuff was overpriced to begin with. And, yes, some of the designs and colors left a lot to be desired (you'll find a lot of orange, purple, and neon greens and blues). But, invariably, the merchandise ends up being sold for pennies on the dollar because its creators began by saying, "Wouldn't it be cool if..." instead of discovering ahead of time whether there was a market for what they wanted to sell.

Tempting though it may be, don't start with a blank piece of paper when you contemplate creating something new. Instead, begin with a market need.

There are at least six reasons you shouldn't start with an idea:

1. **No one other than you might care**. As we have already seen, it is typical for people to start companies to satisfy their own needs or those they have seen or experienced firsthand. You break your arm and you can't believe how itchy the cast is. So you create a new kind of casting material that contains an anti-itch coating on the inside. There is nothing wrong with this approach. It's just that your needs might not be representative of a large enough market to support the idea and/or it may be hard to locate a sufficient number of customers. (See the earlier discussion of Sherlock Holmes cookware.)

2. **There isn't really a need.** I suppose somewhere you can find people who truly hate having their shampoo and conditioner bottles exposed in the shower (even though when you draw the shower curtain no one can see them). And it is more than possible for you to create some kind of waterproof cozy to cover them up. But for the life of me I don't know how you protect the idea from competition—it would be remarkably simple to copy it the moment it came out—or how many people might care about the product. (Really, until I mentioned it, did you ever think about the fact that your shampoo and conditioner bottles are visible?)

3. **People might want your idea, but you simply don't have the resources to make it work.** There is probably a huge market for private shuttle flights to the moon, but what exactly do you know about rocketry (or raising the billions of dollars it is probably going to take to make the idea work?).

4. **People might care, but may not be willing to pay.** See the discussion on the Iridium phone.

5. **People might care, but not all that much.** You may have a truly wonderful idea, but the market may not be big enough to fund the costs of filling it. Here's a simple example. Ever since the first version of Microsoft Office came out, people have complained about Microsoft. The software is not intuitive. It seems to require more clicks than necessary and it makes things harder than they have to be. (Try to do something that should be simple, like paginating a document. If you don't want page 1 to be numbered page 1, you can end up pulling your hair out.) Countless people have said, "You know, Word would be so much better if..." and they begin to fantasize about starting an improved word processing program. The problem? Most people think Word is good enough, and they don't really see a reason to switch, especially not if it means: 1) buying a separate software program and 2) learning how to use a new program that is only incrementally better.

6. **It takes time.** Once you come up with your new idea you have to, as we talked about before, go out and find customers. If you start with a market need, you already have them. They are the people who have said they have a need that they would like you to address.

Planning Is Overrated

Let me tell a quick tale out of school. A couple of years ago, I came up with what I thought was a terrific idea for a book. I would go to successful entrepreneurs and ask them for copies of their original business plans. I'd organize the book by key business insights—marketing, distribution, whatever—and that way potential entrepreneurs could see at a glance what they needed to do to be successful.

There was only one problem with the book concept. Most of the business plans had nothing to do with what the businesses eventually became. People who said they were going to specialize in developing new computer hardware ended up in software, for example. Companies that started with the goal of serving the end consumer became specialists in helping distributors. In a surprisingly high number of cases, the business plan ended up having very little to do with what the (successful) company ultimately became, even if it stayed within the same field.

I never did the book.

Here's the reason I told that story. I know the first sentence of advice to would-be entrepreneurs is usually "create a business plan." But my experience in writing about and learning from entrepreneurs for the past three decades is that creating a painfully detailed business plan really doesn't make much sense (with one limited exception, which I will discuss in a minute).

> If you start with the market need, a huge portion of the market research is done for you. You know a significant number of people who might buy your product. They are the ones who have already told you they need it.

Why doesn't creating a business plan make sense? Because you can plan and research all you want, but the first time you encounter

41

something you didn't expect out in the marketplace—and that is likely to happen on day one—the plan goes out the window. Once you are underway, things never go exactly the way you anticipate. Ah, you say, that means you didn't plan enough. No, not really. It is impossible to make a list ahead of time of all the things you haven't thought of. (Go ahead. Try.)

But the problem with creating a business plan actually starts long before you are underway. The longer you plan, the longer you are not in the marketplace. And that means three things are happening, and none of them are good.

1. No revenues are coming in.
2. There's a possibility that someone could beat you to the punch and introduce your great idea before you do.
3. The market is changing, and as a result you could fall out of step. To use an extreme example to make the point, while you are planning, fine-tuning, and tweaking your plans for making the world's best VCR, the market shifts to DVRs; VCRs go the way of eight-track tapes, typewriters, and printed encyclopedias, and the fact that you have the world's best does you little good.

Given all those reasons, putting together a full-blown business plan doesn't make any sense, unless you need tens of millions of dollars to get underway. If you require that kind of cash, you are going to need to do a business plan. Professional investors will require it, as will your board of directors if you work for a large firm. No one is going to put up tens of millions without a detailed business plan in place.

But few of us need that kind of money. If you don't need millions, do what we talked about in the last chapter. Get out into the marketplace as soon as you can and ask people for an order. If they give it you, you have done all the research necessary. If they don't, ask them why and change your product or service as necessary.

Two Last Thoughts on Plans

As you have seen, I think planning in general—and business plans, in particular—are extremely overrated. It is not that I am against planning. But plans start with the assumption that you can predict the future with a high level of certainty. If you can, then by all means:

1. Forecast the future.
2. Construct a number of plans for achieving what you want, picking the optimal one.
3. Assemble the necessary resources.
4. Go out and implement the plan.

As we discussed earlier, this works well when things in the future are going to be similar to those in the immediate past. For example, if you want to sell an existing product into an adjacent market, this approach works just fine (and you never want to abandon what works).

But, and it is a huge but, the number of extremely predictable situations we all face is decreasing. When you are heading into the unknown, the Act-Learn-Build-Repeat model we talked about in chapter 1 works best. And that model requires action, not planning. You want to get out into the marketplace as quickly as you can and let your customers and potential customers decide if you are on to something.

That said, there are two things you must do before starting anything new. Neglecting them will make your life far more difficult than it has to be. First, make sure you have the requisite desire. And by requisite, I mean a lot. Starting anything new requires overwhelming amounts of passion to get over and through all the inevitable obstacles you are going to face. If this new idea is not something you really want to do, you are not going to give it your all—and that is going to substantially decrease your chances of success.

Second, focus on an area where you feel strong. This is directly related to the first point. At some point as you're getting underway, things are not going to go well. It is at exactly those moments that you have to draw on everything you know to get over the hurdles. Obviously, the better you feel about your skills, the more confidently you can attack the problems.

So make sure these two requirements are in place and figure out how to make your product a success.

Marketing your offering is where we turn our attention next.

Takeaways for Entrepreneurs and the Rest of Us

1. Always, always, always start by solving a market need instead of coming up with a wonderful idea.

2. Make sure the need is real and big enough before getting underway. No, that does not mean elaborate testing. Yes, it means getting some proof before you start.

3. Get underway quickly. Don't wait to perfect your product or service. Launch as quickly as you can and change what the market tells you to change.

CHAPTER 4

The Secret of Marketing? Compete Differently

Starting is scary. Starting means you put yourself—and your money and your reputation—out there and at risk. Starting means you are facing head on the possibility that you may fail, and fail in front of family and friends who may have provided funding for your entrepreneurial venture.

Instead of doing any of those frightening things, it is easier and feels safer to keep thinking and researching your new idea, "just to be sure." But if that is the course you take, you will never start anything. There will always be one more piece of information you will need. One more call you have to make. One more thing that delays pulling the trigger.

As we talked about earlier, you need to get your product out into the marketplace as quickly as possible and see whether it sells. And if you have a service, you want to provide it to customers as quickly as you can, not only to see if people like it but to understand what needs to change.

This does not mean you get your product or service out there under the cover of darkness, though. And that brings us to how you are going to market what you have.

Marketing 101

Marketing, especially as practiced by the best entrepreneurs, is really pretty simple: **you figure out who you want to sell to, and then you determine what will get them to buy.**

That's it.

The way successful entrepreneurs go about marketing is a little more complicated, but not much. There are about a dozen fundamentals the best marketers use to lay the groundwork of a successful marketing campaign. And with those in place, they turn to tactics that increase the chances of success.

Before we deal with the tactics, let's start with the fundamentals that apply to any company of any size.

1. It's all about the customer. Invariably, entrepreneurs find themselves going up against far larger competitors. There is great strength in size, of course. Big companies have more resources to draw on and more expertise. But they also have great weaknesses as well. Big companies are seen as cold, impersonal, and focused on their needs—and those of their shareholders—rather than on customers' needs. The best entrepreneurs always keep the focus on the customer. And large organizations keep trying to become accessible.

2. Focus. I love the way Don Kingsborough, the man behind the success of Teddy Ruxpin and Lazer Tag, explained this to me years ago: "You cannot hire enough people so that you have all the good ideas. That is a bad concept. I think the right concept is to figure out who has the best ideas and figure out what you do best. You concentrate on that, and if someone else has a good idea, buy it and make it successful." People reduce this concept to "find a niche and fill it," but Kingsborough's argument is more nuanced (and clever).

3. Make small bets. This fits in perfectly with the Act-Learn-Build-Repeat model that we talked about earlier. Your resources are limited, and starting anything new is risky. You don't want to compound those risks by betting everything on one roll of the dice.

4. Make those small bets quickly. No, you don't want to lose money. But, since you are not risking much, you can afford a small failure or two. Get out in the marketplace fast and let potential customers tell you if you are on to something. (Again, this is just a variation on my argument that you don't want to spend too much time doing market research.)

5. Understand where to place those small bets (I). Obviously, place bets in areas where competitors don't exist or are weak.

6. Understand where to place those small bets (II). Not so obviously, place bets in areas where you feel strong. That confidence will help you overcome the inevitable hurdles you will face.

In the NFL, offensive coordinators spend Monday and part of Tuesday preparing the game plan for the upcoming week. Then, before they introduce it to the team, they go over it with the starting quarterback. If there is a play or concept the quarterback isn't comfortable with, it is instantly scratched.

Ponder that for a moment. We are talking about incredibly smart, talented athletes, like Tom Brady, Peyton

Manning, Russell Wilson. They have the physical ability to make any throw and the intelligence to master any complex offensive scheme the coordinator creates, yet if they are uncomfortable—for any reason—the play is killed, no matter how hard the coordinator worked on it (or how convinced he is that it would work in the game).

Why? What the smartest people—and that includes successful entrepreneurs as well as NFL quarterbacks and coaches—know is that it is always a good idea to play to your strengths instead of trying to offset your weaknesses. If you feel strongly about a particular situation you will be more confident, and that confidence feeds on itself. Because you know you can do it, you usually will. And if you encounter a problem along the way, you don't get flustered or confused. You calmly start working on a solution. You know there is nothing to worry about. The situation is in your wheelhouse and there isn't an obstacle you can't overcome.

This is, of course, not the usual advice. From grade school on, you have been told to improve the areas where you are weak. Almost no one tells you to do more of what you are good at and ignore everything else (or at least find someone or something that can offset your weakness).

Why not work on your weaknesses? Let's say that you are, on a scale of one to ten, a one when it comes to marketing the product or service you have created. You can work really hard on your marketing—studying things that work, reading articles and books, consulting with consultants—and your skills could improve as a result. You could get up to a three, let's say. The problem with that is, you are still lousy at marketing. (There are people out there who are clearly a ten, and you need to assume you are always competing against tens.) And you have wasted a lot of time that could have been better used building up your strengths.

It is always better to capitalize on what you do best instead of trying to offset your weaknesses. Making a weakness less of a weakness is simply not as good as being the best you can be at something you have an aptitude for.

There are three reasons why that's true:

- By definition, you are bad at the things you are bad at. As we said, we all operate in a competitive marketplace. Why would you want to handicap yourself by concentrating in an area where you gain relatively little?
- Working at things you are not good at is frustrating and saps energy. That makes it harder to build your company.
- You have limited resources. You need to maximize your potential.

So the best entrepreneurs look for opportunities that play to their strengths. And if marketing is not among them, as is the case in our example, good entrepreneurs bring in people who can help them.

The market where they—or the people they bring in— begin to look? One that is underserved by others and yet is big enough to support a business. (See sidebar "Fishing Where the Fish Are.")

7. **There is no formula.** As numerous entrepreneurs told me, you can't use focus groups to create anything new.

Think back to the 1960s, a time when most people had not been exposed to fast food restaurants because there were relatively few. If you asked people where they would like to buy a hamburger, they'll describe a better Howard Johnson's[1] or a restaurant that would serve a better hamburger. They wouldn't invent McDonald's because McDonald's—or what we now think of as McDonald's—was beyond their frame of reference.

Focus groups can't do the work for you; you need to do the heavy lifting yourself. And you need to be involved. But you only have so much time, energy, and ability to focus. That means, as much as you would like to, you can't do everything. That's a given. So is this: the areas that receive your full attention will do better than the areas that don't. It follows, then, that you need to make hard choices about what you will do—and what you won't—when it comes to marketing and everything else. And choosing what you'll commit to is the most important decision you make, because everything else you do will flow from it. So, the question is: Where do you want to spend your time? Your answer may lead to the single most important decision you ever make.

8. Invent a customer. Sometimes, when you are coming up with a new idea, conjuring a fictional customer you are trying to appeal to can help you focus. Leslie H. Wexner, the man who created and built L Brands (formerly Limited Brands) and the Victoria's Secret empire (and there really is no better word)—and who is clearly one of the most successful entrepreneurs of our time—is a master at inventing a prototypical customer.

When he started the Limited stores, Wexner's fictional customer was a Connecticut College student. A few years later, Hollywood gave him the embodiment of the type: Ali MacGraw's character, Jennifer Cavalleri, in *Love Story*. Wexner again fabricated a model customer when he imagined the Victoria's Secret stores. This time the ideal was Cybill Shepherd as Maddie Hayes in the television show *Moonlighting*, which aired from 1985 to 1989 and is remembered, if it is remembered at all, for making Bruce Willis a star. To this day, Wexner doesn't know if MacGraw or

Shepherd ever shopped at one of his stores, but he does know that the fictional women they portrayed were exactly the kind of customers he was trying to attract.

That focus made it easy to decide what to stock. All the merchants had to ask was: "Is this the sort of thing MacGraw or Shepherd's characters would wear?" If it was, it went on the shelf. If it wasn't, it didn't. That guideline kept his businesses remarkably focused. What worked for the highly successful L Brands companies will work for you.

9. Be satisfied with making one significant improvement in a product or service. You're bound to make mistakes attempting just one thing—and you'll make many more if you try to do too much.

10. Keep looking for those limited markets where you have a genuine competitive edge. That's where profitability and security lie. Tempting as it may be, don't try to buy your way into markets where you offer the same product at a lower price. That's where you'll be vulnerable. (See the earlier discussion of why you don't want to compete on price.)

11. Ask for the sale. It seems so fundamental, but it is amazing how many people don't. One business-to-business supplier told me that his company increased sales 10 percent by simply calling people who used to do business with them and asking if they would like to place another order.

12. Create a winning corporate image. Nordstrom means service, Walmart low prices. And when people hear the name of your company, they think of...

In a market in which too many businesses are competing for the same customers, companies must find new ways of letting people know exactly what they stand for. A clear corporate image does that, whether you sell to consumers or to other businesses. Every time you think of McDonald's or McKinsey & Co., an impression—more powerful than any ad—forms in your mind. Customers will judge your company on *everything*, from the dust on the floor to whether your employees snarl. If you go to an F.A.O. Schwarz store you'll end up smiling, which is appropriate. After all, it sells toys. When you walk into the offices of the private banking division of Merrill Lynch or Russell Reynolds Associates, there's no doubt that they are used to dealing with the rich and powerful.

13. You are always better off having a point of difference in your product, instead of coming out with a "me too" and relying on your merchandising and advertising ability. People who say, "We are better marketers than our competitors that's why we will win," are just fooling themselves. People don't buy better marketing. They buy a better product or service, one that improves their lives in some way.

How to Stay Ahead of the Competition

If you are going to satisfy a market need, you have to listen to the market and give people what they want. Sounds obvious, right? But that means you have to evolve if customers tell you to, and that can be difficult. After all, you have spent time identifying market need X. You have raised money, laid out a sales and distribution plan, and figured out exactly what you need to do to make X a reality. And then, all of a sudden, the market says X is not such a good idea, or Y would be better.

Can you change in that sort of situation? If you can't, you are doomed; you don't need to look at further than the fate of Blockbuster video or the publishers of printed encyclopedias to see that.

Question: What does this mean for you and your organization?

Answer: You need to stay one step ahead of the competition.

Let's talk about five ideas you can use to do just that.

1. **Scan the horizon and develop the skills you will need.** The phrase "continuous learning" has become a cliché, and that's too bad. Being a one-trick pony doesn't do you any good when the market is tired of your trick. You always have to be learning new skills to satisfy evolving customer needs. What customers want will also change over time, and you have to change with them.

2. **Cross-train.** Just like you, everyone in your organization needs to be flexible and adaptable.

3. **Commit to few fixed costs.** The deeper the roots, the harder it is to move. Keep that thought in mind before making any large expenditures.

4. **Refresh your workforce constantly.** Organizations can get set in their ways, just like people do. One simple way to overcome that tendency is to constantly hire new people. And if those people are younger than you are, so much the better. To a dinosaur like me, there is something comforting about watching people in their twenties and thirties cope with change in general and the constant upheaval in technology in particular. For example, I have

yet to meet someone under twenty-five who isn't comfortable using countless office productivity programs or who can't navigate her way around a Mac or PC. (I think of these young employees as being bilingual.)

5. **Embrace diversity.** Speaking of bilingual ability, what have you done to respond to the fact that the United States will, in the foreseeable future, be a majority-minority country? (I am amazed that every consumer product website is *not* available in English and Spanish.)

None of these five things is particularly easy to do. But they all need to be done, if you want to stay ahead of the competition.

Remember what I said at the outset of this chapter. After they lay the foundation for successful marketing (by doing the things we just talked about), the best entrepreneurs move on to tactics.

What is so interesting is that the basic tactics haven't changed since I first compiled the following list thirty years ago. Oh, the way entrepreneurs go about doing it (via the web; as a smartphone app) has changed. But the list itself is the same. Here are ten ways you can compete differently to find a hole in the marketplace:

1.   **Upgrade.** Take a basic product and make it special, either by adding value to it or by marketing it as a status product. Private jet ownership is one example. So is the whole artisanal movement—pickles, cheeses, you name it fits here as well. In each case, the underlying concept remains unchanged but the product's image has been improved. You are still flying from point A to point B, you are just doing it without fellow passengers. The pickle or cheese is still a pickle or cheese but it isn't mass produced.

2. Downgrade. Take a product that has always been associated with status and reduce it to its underlying concept. For example, in the 1980s People Express Airlines eliminated all the frills that came with an airplane ticket (meals, magazines, etc.) and reduced flight to simple transportation. The Wright brothers didn't show movies aboard when they took off from Kitty Hawk, and neither did People Express, one of the first discount airlines. Some thirty years later all the major airlines are, unfortunately, copying the People Express model, but still charging full fare. The "generic" products you can find in every supermarket aisle are another example.

3. Bundle. There are certain products or services that it just makes sense to combine. A camera with a cell phone is a great example. People take their phones everywhere and they often want to capture a memory of what is right in front of them. Sure, you can find better stand-alone cameras, and yes, there are higher-quality cell phones that come without cameras, but the combined units work well—and make consumers happy. (Bundling has become commonplace in technology of all kinds. For example, printers come with built-in scanners.)

4. Unbundle. This is the flip side of what we discussed above. What products have been so gussied up that you could break them down and sell the individual components? The easiest example of this is life insurance. It became common practice in the industry to combine the protection component with a savings element. That became the basic insurance policy. Term insurance, which eliminates the savings component and just provides protection, has become very popular.

But there are other, more subtle examples. Television "spin-offs," which take a popular supporting character from one show and create a new program centering on that character, would qualify. So, too, would taking a section of a magazine (say the "People" section of *Time* magazine) and creating a freestanding publication.

5. Transport. If a product sells in one area, take it to another. If you stop and think about it, that is what importing and exporting are all about. But you can transport ideas as well. Trends that originate one place—the big cities on the coasts—can be introduced to the heartland, for example. Think of all the stores and products on the East Coast than contain the word "California" in their names. And then head out to the West Coast and count the products and places that say "New York-style." In Las Vegas, they are not even subtle about it, with venues like the New York-New York Hotel and Casino and the Paris Las Vegas.

6. Mass market. Take an idea that has succeeded in a narrow area and see if it will scale. It is hard to believe now, when there are more than 18,000 stores in 115 countries, but for the longest time—up until the late 1960s—it was virtually impossible to find a Kentucky Fried Chicken restaurant outside the South. The chain, now called, KFC (and countless other franchisors) took its regional success and kept expanding into new geographic markets.

Once upon a time, the people who made extra-virgin olive oil only sold through gourmet shops. Today, you can find endless varieties in Walmart and Sam's Clubs.

7. Narrowcast. We borrow the term from television. When cable television was in its infancy its broadcasters realized they shouldn't all try to reach mass audiences. For all their faults, the three networks did a fairly good job of serving the widest audience possible (even if they do occasionally offer shows like *Me and the Chimp*).

The solution for cable operators was to narrowcast, or gear shows on a given channel to a particular audience. So you have channels that show nothing but sports or classic movies. Not only is there a hugely popular all-weather station, there are channels devoted to specific religions.

8. Think big. Instead of carrying just one product, carry everything related to it. Think of "big-box stores" like Sam's Club or a super-sized golf store.

9. Think small. While huge stores can offer more merchandise, they don't usually have the high-end stuff that a certain percentage of the population demands. And their service, to be kind, is often lacking.

10. Price. At first blush, you may not think of competing on price as niche finding, but it is. Remember, we are talking about competing differently, and price is clearly one way to differentiate yourself from your competitors.

Competing on price is extremely difficult to do. After all, only one company can truly have the lowest price, and if all you do is tie them, customers will look for another point of differentiation. The net result: you will end up in the same place you are now, but with substantially lower margins. No wonder everyone—including me—recommends against it.

However, in some ridiculously competitive industries you have no choice. Or you really think it is the way to go in order to stand out. Or...Whatever your motivation, if you want to compete on price, let me give you four ways to do it well.

You can offer more value—real or perceived—at a higher price. If everyone is selling blue jeans for $45 a pair, and you make yours fit more snugly around the seat and charge $75, you are offering more (perceived?) value at a higher price. And even if it costs a bit more to make those jeans fit better, you are substantially ahead of the game when it comes to profits.

Offer more value for the same money. Your competitors are offering a gallon of perfectly good paint for $17.99. If you sell a longer-lasting, better-quality paint at the same price, you are offering more value for the same money.

You can offer less quality at a much lower price. The competition sells tires that last 50,000 miles for $100 apiece. You sell a tire that will last only 25,000 miles, 50 percent as long, for $40, or some 60 percent cheaper. You are offering less value at a lower price.

You can offer the same value at a lower price. Everyone sells tea kettles at $7.99. If you can sell the same-quality kettle for $6.99, you are offering the same value at a lower price.

I am not advocating that you compete on price. But if it is a marketing strategy you choose, these ideas can help—and keep you profitable.

Just remember previous warnings about how dangerous a strategy this can be.

Fishing Where the Fish Are

I am, at heart, "a magazine guy." I had my own subscription to *Sports Illustrated* when I was eight. I spent years writing a column for the *New York Times* about magazine stories people might have missed, and, of course, I spent a good portion of my life as a staff writer for national business magazines.

So it is probably not surprising that a few summers back I paid more attention than most when *Esquire* did a cover story entitled: "How to Be a Man: A Guide to Your 20s, 30s, 40s, and 50s...After That You Are on Your Own."

Being in my fifties, I got the joke. But then I got to wondering. *Esquire* is going after males in their twenties to their fifties. So is *GQ*. And *Men's Health*. And *Men's Journal*. And

Playboy. And *Penthouse*. And *Sports Illustrated*. And...If anything, those magazines will tell you they're targeting readers at the lower end of the twenty-to-fifty age range—where they run headlong into publications such as *Maxim, Stuff, Details, HFM*...This is an awfully competitive marketplace.

The same dynamic plays out on the distaff side of the magazine rack. There are a huge number of publications—everything from *Allure, Cosmo,* and *Elle* to *Vogue*—designed for women eighteen to forty-nine.

My guess is that the way magazines target their audience isn't a whole lot different from the way you target your potential market.

You know why advertisers are targeting these people:

1. There are an awful lot of them.
2. In the aggregate, they have a bunch of money that they presumably can spend with the companies that advertise.
3. If you get customers when they are young, you stand to make substantial profits as they (hopefully) continue buying your product over their lifetimes.

But does any of this really make sense? Maybe not.

While it is true that there are a lot of people age twenty to forty-nine, some 42 percent of the population according to the Census Bureau, you have to wonder how much money they actually have. Most folks in their thirties and forties are raising kids, and there goes the whole concept of discretionary income.

But the bigger question is whether you want to fight everyone else to reach the same people. If you've ever watched a golf tournament on TV you instantly understand the problem. Every commercial break is filled with ads for Acuras, Audis, BMWs, Cadillacs, Infinitis, Lexuses, Mercedes....Sure, if you are selling a luxury car, you want to reach an upscale audience like those the golf tournaments provide. But if you are doing exactly the same thing the competition is—advertising where rich people gather—what edge do you have?

Wouldn't it be better to fish where there are fewer fishermen? No, I am not talking about niche markets, but about underserved audiences.

Staying with our magazine theme, that is exactly what *More*, a magazine aimed at women over forty, does. With a circulation of 1.3 million readers a month, which is about twice that of *Esquire*, this women's magazine does a solid job, month after month, delivering what its audience wants. Articles such as "Is It Ever Too Late to Find Faith?" and "The Joy of Accepting Our Curves" (where women who are never going to be described as having a model-like figure pose and discuss body issues) are not everyone's cup of tea. But that is exactly the point. *More* is fishing in an under-fished pond.

Doesn't it make sense that you should go searching for (a lot of) customers where your competition isn't looking?

Creating Customers for Life

As we have seen, competing differently boils down to where you choose to spend your time and money. Instead of investing in marketing and advertising campaigns, many of the best entrepreneurs on the planet—such as L.L. Bean—spend their energy and money satisfying customers. If you can turn a onetime buyer into a life-time customer, six things happen, all of them good.

1. **Your sales go up.** People have a real reason for doing business with you. You have done a good job of taking care of them, and that is a more effective way to get customers to stick with you than any ad you can run or clever Internet marketing campaign you can design.

2. **If you are helped (your sales go up), the competition is hurt (their sales go down).** Customers only have so much money to spend. If people are spending money with you, they are not spending that same money with the people you are competing against.

3. **They stay with you longer.** Acquiring customers is an expensive undertaking. If you take care of your existing customers, they have fewer reasons to leave you, which of course decreases your marketing costs.

4. **Loyalty builds a barrier to competition.** If you have done a good job taking care of your customers, it is going to be difficult for your competition to lure them away. You have to keep taking care of them, of course. But if you do, customers will stick with you.

5. **It is easier to get customers to buy more.** This is simply the flip side of the previous point. It is always easier to sell additional products and services to people with whom you already have a good relationship. You don't need to establish a level of trust that will make them feel comfortable in buying. You already have it.

6. **You can achieve higher margins.** If you have made your customers happy, they will be willing to pay a bit more for what you offer. You can't gouge them, of course, but they will be a bit

less price sensitive. Most people really do believe, as I do, that you get what you pay for.

How to Create Those Customers for Life

You are convinced that customer service can be an effective business strategy, so what is the first thing that you do? That's simple. You ask customers what they want and you give it to them. Both parts of that sentence are equally important.

You have to ask because you don't define customer service, and I don't either. The only person who does is your customer. That's why you have to ask your customers what they want.

And once they tell you, you have to provide it (for free, if possible; at a fair price if it is not). Starting down the road to providing excellent service really is as simple as that, and the nice thing is that it feeds upon itself.

A. If you are good to your customers, they will come back.
B. If they come back, they are likely to spend more.
C. If they spend more, you will treat them better.
D. If you treat them better, they will come back—and the cycle continues.

Using customer service as one of your primary marketing tools can be extremely profitable.

No Advertising or PR—Share Instead

I swear I am not making this up. I was sitting in my boss's office at *Inc.*, the magazine devoted to writing about growing companies, when the phone rang. It was a public relations woman from multibillion-dollar Warner-Lambert Co. She wanted to know when

Inc. was going to do that story she pitched on the company's new flavor of Trident gum.

The boss was a patient man, so he explained that (1) we are the magazine for growing companies—it says so right on the cover—and Warner-Lambert is many things, but it ain't no growth company, and (2) everything we publish is designed to help owners and managers of growing companies do their jobs better. "Given that," the boss asked, "why would a story on Trident interest our readers?"

Said the PR woman, "They chew gum, don't they?"

That story explains in a nutshell what's wrong with public relations firms and why most of the best small companies handle PR efforts themselves. It also underscores why larger companies may want to rethink their public relations budgets.

Many public relations firms haven't a clue about what would interest the audience they're pitching, and they rarely listen when a reporter or editor tries to explain it to them. If they did, we never would have received, while I was at *Inc.,* requests for coverage of the International Llama Association's ninth annual convention or of the completion of a new bridge linking Georgia and South Carolina. Nor would we have received a news release in Spanish pitching (we think) a new sitcom on Telemundo.

These examples would be funny, except for two things. First, odds are, your public relations folks are guilty of sending out equally inappropriate information. Just ask for the list of media that received your last press release. You'll be amazed. And second, it's a waste of a great deal of money.

That's why the most successful entrepreneurs don't do traditional public relations or advertising. The best do some variation of the very successful approach that Alison Davis, founder and president of Davis & Company, does. She runs a thirty-person New Jersey–based firm that helps Fortune 200 companies do a better job of communicating with their employees, and her marketing is as focused as the advice she offers to clients.

Davis has created an e-newsletter than goes to just about every large company in the United States, and it is filled with tips, suggestions, and best practices. Her marketing people work hard to book her for speaking engagements in front of audiences filled with the decision makers who can hire her firm, and she blogs and writes books in her field of expertise, which raises her company's profile even further.

She has found this far more effective than any traditional marketing or PR she could do, and it is a strategy that large companies could adopt on a massive scale, sending their senior executives out to do more speeches before groups that could turn out to be clients. The focus for Davis is on building her business, a concept we will expand upon in detail in the next chapter.

Takeaways for Entrepreneurs and The Rest of Us

1. **At the highest level, marketing is remarkably simple:** you figure out who you want to sell to, and then you determine how you are going to get those people to buy.

2. **Listen, listen, and listen some more.** The only people who determine whether you are on to something with your new product or service is your customers. If they say you need to improve or change something about your offering, do it.

3. **Customer service is not a "nice to have."** It must be an essential part of your business strategy.

CHAPTER 5

Don't Set Out to Become Rich

When the subject of successful entrepreneurs and their riches comes up, we all have our favorite images. For some, it is owner of the Virgin empire (records, airlines, space travel) Sir Richard Branson and his private seventy-four-acre isle in the British Virgin Islands. (You can rent the island, which comes complete with accommodations for thirty, for about $60,000 a night.) Others love the idea that the riches that come from creating a successful company allow you to follow just about any whim. Jeff Bezos, founder of Amazon, bought the *Washington Post*, overpaying substantially when he wrote a $250 million check.

My favorite image relating to entrepreneurial riches was a picture in the *New York Times* on the day after Twitter went public. There were a handful of men—and they were all men—staring up at a stock ticker that showed how much Twitter stock (TWTR in Wall Street shorthand) was trading for moments after going public (the stock was already climbing steadily). The picture of the normal-looking guys was nothing out of the ordinary—just a bunch of white guys standing around gawking—but the caption *was.* It identified the men in the photo and the amount of money in *billions* each had just made from the public offering.

I am not alone in being fascinated by pictures like that. There is no doubt that, when people think of successful entrepreneurs, one of the first things that comes to mind. It is a relatively quick jump to "I am going to start a company so I can get rich." (Or, "I am going to help my established company make a substantial profit, so I can share in the windfall.")

One of the smartest, most successful guys I know understands that leap, and he is quick to point out why it is wrong.

> When starting a company, don't set out to become rich. If that is your goal, odds are you will be disappointed. Instead, set a commercial goal and accomplish it. You will become rich as a by-product.

He responds with an interesting question when people ask him if they should start a business. "I ask if they want to make a million dollars," he begins. "Everybody always says yes, but they are answering the wrong question. What they mean by yes, is yes, they would like to have a million dollars, a house on the ocean, and all that. They don't necessarily want to earn it. The hard part is building a business to the point where you have that million dollars. But that is also the part that is the most fun." To people like my buddy, a millionaire many times over, what's important is translating their visions into reality. That's why they start companies, not to become rich. Wealth is just a pleasant by-product.

That's why, as we discussed earlier in the book, the best entrepreneurs don't wait for inspiration to strike or until they come up with a truly original idea. (My friend, trained as a lawyer, made his money initially by buying and selling strip malls before branching out into complex real estate transactions and later into buying whole businesses.) If you wait until you have a completely original idea or an "important" idea, you will wait forever to take the entrepreneurial plunge. As we have seen, truly original ideas are hard to come by and, even worse, they take a long time to explain to your potential market, which prevents you from getting underway.

It's far better to come up with a variation on something that already exists. Then establish a commercial goal and set off to accomplish it. The most successful entrepreneurs do just that. As we said earlier, they all looked at the market and then tried to fill a need, based on their own individual strengths. Both components—the market's need and your ability to accomplish it—must be present if the idea is to work.

What almost never works is starting a company simply because you want to become rich.

Let's talk about why.

The Road to Failure

Think for a minute about the thousands of "entrepreneurs" who planned to make millions selling computer software as the personal computer boom hit or by renting movies for videocassette and Blu-ray players or by capitalizing on the cupcake craze. Very few of them ever made a dollar let alone became wealthy. They failed for the same reason get-rich-quick schemes always fail. These "entrepreneurs" plunged into a hot market, where, by definition, the competition is fiercest, and they weren't prepared.

Carried away with the thought of becoming rich instantly, they didn't take the time to study their competition or even determine what the market really wanted. To say, as people did at the beginning of the personal computer boom, that "everyone is going to need software—I'll open a store," is meaningless. What people? Personal computer users or business owners? What software? Programs for high-end personal computers or for game machines? The list of questions they didn't ask is endless. Should I discount? Sell by mail? Sell more than software? Is being a distributor, rather than a retailer, actually a better way to go? Perhaps the most basic questions of all were: Do I understand this market? Does what I have decided to do play to my strengths? What exactly is going to be my competitive advantage?

Most of the people who owned the quickly shuttered computer software stores never asked these questions. Their only goal was to make a lot of money in a short amount of time. And without the discipline of establishing a commercial goal and then methodically setting off to accomplish it, that will never happen.

Really? You Shouldn't Try to be Rich?

If you are having trouble with the idea that wealth should be a by-product of what you are trying to create, and not the primary (or even secondary) goal, you are not alone. For the longest time I had the same problem. In fact, my confusion started before I was ever interested in business. It began when I was a sports-obsessed kid, and it continued into my professional life.

I just couldn't understand the overarching philosophy of two of the greatest college coaches I have ever seen. Neither UCLA's John Wooden, perhaps the best basketball coach on any level at any time, nor Nick Saban, the head football coach at Alabama, ever talked about winning when they were asked about what they try to accomplish with their programs. Their focus, they said, was on getting their teams to constantly improve and to always concentrate on doing the right things. If they did those two things, both coaches argued, the wins would follow. Eventually, I understood what they were saying. Their records—Wooden's was 664–162 and Saban is 165–56–1 in college—and all the national championships they won (Wooden: ten, Saban: four) proves they were right to concentrate on the details and not the result, which they believed would take care of itself.

And I got confirmation of their approach when I began looking at the track records of the most successful entrepreneurs. The best ones don't have making a fortune—winning in the eyes of most people—as their goal when they start off. Instead, they did indeed, as we have discussed, go about finding a market need and filling it to the best of their ability.

Why not focus on gaining wealth? Well, in addition to all the problems we have already talked about, if your primary objective is to get rich quick, you are bound to cut corners, shortchange your customers, and fail to take the time to truly understand the market needs. And that, by the way, is true whether you are trying to get your company off the ground or are introducing a new product or service in order to make this quarter's numbers within an established firm. It is simply the wrong path to take.

If you don't understand what the market wants, you are making your life far harder than it has to be. But if you are correct in identifying a market need and have the ability to fill it, riches—just like winning for Wooden and Saban—are the natural by-product of doing everything it takes to satisfy a customer the first time, every time.

The moral: if you focus on doing the right things—and succeed at doing them—you will be rewarded. You need to look no further than Michael Bloomberg, Phil Knight, Sam Walton, Mark Zuckerberg...

But What About Cash Flow?

"Ah, but you are missing the point," some people invariably say when I begin arguing against riches as the primary focus of any new endeavor. "Yes, of course, I would like to have the money. But the real reason I want the funds is to have more than enough resources to make my business a success. That's why I need to make a lot of money in a hurry."

I understand that position. Now, let me argue in favor of constraints and a lack of sufficient resources. Sometimes, to jumpstart the process of innovation, leaders will say to their people, "If money weren't an object, what would you do to improve our company?" (Or create a new product or generate a new service.)

That question might spur creativity, but you need to realize the construct is just silly. Money is always an object. Resources are always limited. Time is always of the essence. You almost never have all the resources you need. You need to deal with the world as it is, if you want to be successful.

If you let creativity go unfettered—that is, if you say, "If money (or time, or whatever) is no object"—you are going to get wonderful ideas. People will talk about robots that can do Excel spreadsheets, travel via antigravity running shoes, and cups and plates that get into the dishwasher by themselves at the end of a meal. Those are lovely ideas, but they're not particularly helpful to anyone but fiction writers because none of them is going to be practical anytime soon.

You need to tether creativity to business goals. More specifically, you need to make sure all those wonderful thoughts and all that innovation you are encouraging leads to a potentially profitable venture. Creativity that isn't tied directly to making money is simply a waste of time. It might be a fun hobby when you are off the clock, but it does you little good at work, especially if that work is creating something new.

That's why all the constraints you face when you are trying to get underway are a good thing. You can ask, "Given the situation we have, what can we do to satisfy a very specific customer need?" That way, everyone is focusing her most creative thoughts on ideas that can lead to money-making ventures instead of on math-geek robots.

And I will go further. **I think having too much money in the early days of building a business, whether you are building it for**

yourself or for someone else, is a bad thing. Of course I know the counterargument, which boils down to: "Money is good. And the more money, the better. Having a lot of money allows you to move faster, and if you fail it's no big deal. There will be additional funds where those came from."

And that is exactly the problem. Having too much money can be a liability. Not a huge one, but a liability nonetheless. Think back to the Act-Learn-Build-Repeat model we talked about in chapter 1. Explicit in the model is the requirement that you take small steps, because you want to move quickly and you don't want to waste resources like time or money. Wasting money isn't a problem in and of itself, if you have lots of it. The problem is what it does to your timetable and the efficiency of your actions.

Think about it. If money is not an issue, you may decide to say that there is no need to take small steps. Why bother learning what the market wants? You have enough money to see if your hunch is right. Full speed ahead.

Making large leaps with unlimited funds is certainly an approach you can take. It just isn't a very wise one. You always want to be solving for a market need. Having less money forces you to do that. It also makes you more creative. Having money is a good thing. But not having it is not as big a liability as you might think.

Getting Paid

High on the list of things that people *don't* think about when starting a business is how they are going to get paid. If you are typical, you figure you'll do the work or ship the product or provide the service, send out a bill, and a check will come a few days later.

Given that receivables rarely work that way, entrepreneurs have to learn what works—and what doesn't—when it comes to getting the money they are owed. Here are nine ideas that work.

1. **Don't have any receivables at all.** Everybody has his own formula, but the common denominator is that a good entrepreneur tries to get as much money as he can before work begins, be it 25 percent, 33 percent, 50 percent, or some other number. The bigger the number, the less needs to be collected later, obviously.

2. **Get the whole thing up front**. This can happen if the client is big enough and you offer a substantial discount for being paid in full before work begins. (There are many precedents for this. High-end hotels—such as the Fairmont chain—offer up to a third off if you pay for your room in advance.) The arrangement works especially well if you have a stellar reputation, so the client doesn't have to worry about you doing what you promised.

3. **No money? No work.** Violating this rule is the first thing most entrepreneurs mention when asked about the one lesson they learned the hard way.

The following story, from an entrepreneur who didn't want to be named, is representative: "A new client—who came highly recommended—asked me do a rush job for a lot of money. 'I will pay you right after I set up a new LLC that will be responsible for this project,' he said. I worked really hard for a month and turned in quality work that the client liked, only to be told a couple of days later, 'You know what? I am not going to pursue this idea anymore.' He never set up the LLC and I have yet to be paid. I hope

I have learned my lesson. From now on, I will require a large check up front."

4. **Offer easy installments**. The shorter the intervals between when you do the work and when you get paid, the better your cash flow position. Service providers typically bill half up front and half when the work is done. But why not even bill more frequently, say every time 10 percent of the work is completed, or even 8.5 percent when one-twelfth of the work is done? If clients object to the frequency, you can always suggest that they pay the entire cost of the project immediately, in exchange for a discount. (See the second point.)

5. **Send bills immediately**. No matter what option you go with—25 percent, 10 percent, or even 8.5 percent—send the bill the moment you hit the agreed-upon benchmark. Clients will never pay as fast you would like them to. That means there is going to be a lag in getting paid (more on that in a second). There is no reason to compound it by waiting on your end.

6. **Follow up faster than you think necessary**. Service providers and consultants typically send bills marked "Due immediately," which clients read as "Pay when you feel like it." It is not tacky to start following up within ten days of sending the bill. That follow-up doesn't have to be anything fancy. It could be nothing more than an e-mail with the subject line "Just checking on the check." And, again, if the client objects to the note or to the frequency of the follow-ups, offer a discount if they pay what is owed in the next forty-eight hours.

7. **Make your follow-ups personal**. My favorite version was from the entrepreneur who sent out notes that read: "If it were up to me, I wouldn't be sending these reminders about payments. But since the bursar at College X, where my kid is now a sophomore, has no sense of humor when it comes to late payments, I would sure appreciate it if you could send payment as quick as you can."

8. **Keep following up** . . . every ten days at least.

9. **If a company offers an automatic payment option, take it.** And do so even if in exchange the company takes a small discount—it is usually 2 percent. The discount is not onerous and typically the money is wired to your account on the day promised.

I have a couple of other thoughts about this. People who write about this subject invariably suggest that you use phrases like "2 percent discount if you pay within thirty days" and they advocate adding an interest charge if bills are paid late. I am not a fan of either approach.

If your customers want a discount they'll ask for it during the initial conversation about how much the work is going to cost. Invariably, clients will take the 2 percent discount and pay when they want to anyway. Odds are, you are not going to fight over that 2 percent that they are not entitled to.

As for charging interest, that seems like imposing a penalty, and that is not a particularly good way to stay in your customers' good graces. Getting the money you are owed is hard enough without alienating people by exacting penalties.

If Riches Are So Important...

There is a certain irony in thinking that people start companies to become rich. I have never seen studies on this, but just about every entrepreneur I know is very conservative with her personal investments.

That is surprising to a lot of people but it is true, and you can prove it to yourself. The next time you meet an entrepreneur, ask him this very personal question: "How do you invest your own money?" Most people expect the entrepreneur to say, "I put every dime I have into the business" and for him to add, "if I have anything left over then I invest in the start-ups of my friends." The reality is far different, however.

Entrepreneurs' investment portfolios look like your grandmother's, filled with bonds and cash. They know that starting a business has a certain amount of risk, no matter how careful you are, so they try to offset that risk by following the Act-Learn-Build-Repeat model we talked about, and then further offset that risk by being extremely conservative with their personal investments.

If you think about it for a second, this isn't surprising. After all, starting something new is in large part beyond your control, and why would you want to double down on risk by making speculative investments with the money that isn't tied up in your business? As one entrepreneur told me, "I am already over-indexed on risky investments, my company. Why would I want to compound that?" A conservative approach is simply prudent.

How to Make More Money

But the question remains, is there a way to make more money without taking any more risks with your investments? There is. It isn't difficult. It just takes discipline and a quick review of the basics.

Since we are talking about increasing returns on investment, that is the place to start, with the formula that determines ROI. You know the formula:

$$\frac{\text{Income (gain on investment} - \text{cost of investment)}}{\text{Investment}} = \text{ROI}$$

Let's deal with the way ROI is traditionally used in business—to make sure we are all on the same page—then we will show you how you can think about it differently when it comes to your personal investments, so you can generate more income without increasing your risk. When businesses talk about increasing ROI, the focus is invariably on the denominator: How can we maintain our current level of earnings (or raise them) yet make less of an investment? Asking the question that way makes perfect sense, of course, because it allows you to increase your profits substantially. It's a great way to make a lot of money.

Let's say your company receives $20 in earnings for every $18 in investment it makes. (Add a whole lot more zeroes to both the top and bottom lines if you think the example is too simplistic.)

$$\frac{\$20 \text{ Income}}{\$18 \text{ Investment}} = 11.11\% \text{ ROI}$$

Your return on investment is 11 percent. But if you find a way to cut investment by just $1 and still get that same $20 in earnings, your return jumps to almost 18 percent.

$$\frac{\$20 \text{ Income}}{\$17 \text{ Investment}} = 17.6\% \text{ ROI}$$

...and with that result, you look like a hero.

That's why everyone thinks about cutting costs (i.e., investment) when the discussion turns to increasing corporate ROI.

How does this affect you and your investments? That's simple. All we have to do is flip the emphasis in the formula. As we have seen, the formula has three parts: income, investment, and ROI. Traditionally, you would try to increase your yield—the numerator. You have $100,000 to invest and if you get 7.5 percent return on your money instead of 6 percent, you would make $7,500, or an extra $1,500 a year. So far, so good.

But, suppose you are the typical entrepreneur and don't want to take the increased risk that comes with chasing increased yield? (And it is always the case that the higher the yield, the higher the risk.) Another way to increase the amount of money you earn is by increasing the denominator—the amount of the investment. Instead of investing $100,000, suppose you got that number up to $125,000 and you earned that same 6 percent you were making before. Your yield would be $7,500—.06 x $125,000—**and you haven't taken any more risk.**

True, this way you have to work a bit harder to save more money. But you will have increased your return without adding any risk.

Weighing the Risks

The discussion of risk brings us to the one last question that must be answered when you are starting a company, or anything new, for that matter. That question is simply: Is it worth the risk?

If getting rich is not the goal—and it's not—then it could be a long while before you have sufficient income coming in to justify the investment of time and money it will take to get things going. And, of course, there is the very real risk that the venture may never be successful. What this means, to be blunt, is this: If you can't afford to follow your passion, then don't quit your day job. But even if that is the case, do keep working on your great idea whenever you can. Even a few minutes a day spent doing what you love is good for you for many reasons—your mental health among them—and you can keep moving forward slowly until you are in a better position to pursue your dream full time.

But what if you really want to pursue your passion full time right now, as a new business venture, a new career, or a new way of life? How do you know if it's the right time to go for it? When will it ever be the right time? How much money (time, resources, investors, etc.) do you have to have before you're ready to go out and just do it?

Everyone will have a different answer to this question, of course, because everyone has a different level of risk that she is comfortable with. But let me give you a rule of thumb: before you do anything, determine your "acceptable loss." You need to know how much you're willing to lose before you begin thinking about starting something new. And you need to do everything possible to make sure you don't exceed that figure.

This is a variation on risk management, of course. If you're going to play in a game with uncertain outcomes, you never want to risk more than you can afford to lose and you want to make sure the potential reward is worth it. Both these ideas are summed up with the word "acceptable."

As you can see, employing the concept of acceptable loss keeps any failures small. By definition, you never lose more than you can afford. What you're willing to risk is clearly defined.

But the concept also gets you to think about other potential costs and losses—not just the financial ones. In fact, there are at least five classes of assets at your disposal and at risk when you start anything new.

1. **Money.** This is the most obvious, of course.

2. **Time.** You want to guard your time just as much as you guard your money. So just as you have a dollar figure that you think would be "acceptable" to lose, you want to have a time limit as well. "I am willing to give this idea up to six months to see if it will work."

3. Professional reputation. We all have one, although when you are first starting out, it may be extremely slight. There is nothing wrong with failing if the idea you tried was worthy and you were sufficiently committed to it. You gave it your best shot. It didn't work. These things happen. On to the next idea.

But if you are seen as someone who doesn't anticipate obvious problems or who can't conserve resources and use them properly, that failure can seriously hurt you in whatever you do next. You may find it far harder to raise money or even to get another opportunity. Damage to your professional reputation can be a huge loss.

4. Personal reputation. People may hate the question "What do you do for a living?" arguing (correctly) that they are more than their job. Still, how people see you is, in part, shaped by how you earn your income. You don't want your new venture to be an embarrassment which could affect your self-esteem or fail to represent who you truly are.

This kind of loss is similar to a loss of professional reputation, but it hits much closer to home. Losing your standing with those near and dear to you can be devastating.

5. Missed opportunities. If you are working to start venture X, you cannot be working on venture Y at exactly the same moment; and Y, potentially, could be a far better idea. In business, this is known as an "opportunity cost"—it's the cost of not pursuing other things that could prove to be even more worthwhile. You want to be mindful of what you are choosing not to do, and you also want to recognize another form of opportunity cost: the price to be paid for not acting right away—someone else might conceive and implement your idea while you are dithering. The price to be paid for that inaction? You might spend the rest of your life in a job you hate or miss a great opportunity to make a once-in-a-lifetime contribution.

Acceptable loss does not depend on the venture but on the individual. It varies from person to person and across the course of an individual's lifetime. (For example, you may be willing to risk more when you're young, knowing you'll have decades to recover should things go wrong; less when your kids are approaching college age and you need to save every dollar you can for those upcoming tuition bills; and then more later once those bills are behind you.)

When it comes to determining how much you can personally risk in following your passion or starting a new venture—that is, your own acceptable loss—ask yourself these questions:

- What are my assets?
- What can I afford to lose?
- What am I willing to lose in the worst-case scenario?

After you think all this through, if you become convinced that you can't succeed for technical, market, or personal reasons, such as exceeding your acceptable loss, then it's not the right time to quit your day job. But, by using the concept of acceptable loss, you may be able to eventually come closer to your dream than you think, by keeping your risk at a manageable level.

This approach doesn't guarantee you will become rich, but it could get you on your way. And once you are, you need to pay attention to your profit and loss statement. Financing is the subject of our next chapter.

Takeaways for Entrepreneurs and the Rest of Us

1. **Strange as it sounds, if making a lot of money is important to you...don't set out to become rich.** Focus on making customers happy. If you do, the money will follow.

2. Prove it to yourself. Pick the ten richest people you can think of and search their online bios. You will inevitably find that becoming rich was never a motivating force for them.

3. Don't wait until you have a lot of money in hand before you start something new. You can probably get underway with a lot less money than you think.

CHAPTER 6

You Need Less Money Than You Think

You are thinking of starting your own company. How much money do you need to get underway? As the Kauffman Foundation, the world's largest foundation devoted to entrepreneurship, notes, "the answer, of course, depends on what kind of company you are starting. If someone is starting a pharmaceutical company to test a new drug, or a FedEx-like gigantic venture, he or she likely will require millions of dollars to get started. If a writer is starting a new blog service, or a developer is launching a new app, the cost is almost zero, except his or her living expenses."[1]

With that by way of background, guess what it costs to get the average company underway. When we factor in every kind of start-up there is—from a lawyer hanging out his own shingle to a new biotech company incorporating—how much money does it take to start a new company?

A. $109,016
B. $484,371

C. $921,823

D. $3,125,411

This should have been easy, because I gave a huge hint in chapter 1. The answer is "A," $109,016, and that is actually rounding up. The number in many cases is a lot less. And that is **the key takeaway from this chapter: you will probably need a lot less money than you think to get underway.** And that is true whether you are starting your own company or beginning a new operation for an established firm.

Just about every book devoted to start-ups spends an inordinate amount of time on financing.[2] I am not going to give it much more than this one short chapter because I think the emphasis is misplaced. If you are going to need less money than you think— and I am going to explain why that is the case in just a moment— then there is no reason to beat the subject to death. Just like we said earlier when we were talking about planning, the subject is overrated.

What's the proof that you probably won't need as much money as you think? Let's go back to the study we talked about in the chapter opening. The Kauffman Foundation tracked 4,928 firms' start-up costs and found the average to be $109,016. (To underscore the point that it may cost you less than that, the figure was $44,793 for firms without employees and $58,448 for home-based companies.) "None of these figures are negligible amounts, but arguably they are not insurmountable obstacles," the foundation noted.

And I cannot stress that enough. When you talk to people who have been reluctant to start their own business, one of the reasons they invariably cite is the cost. True, $109,016 ain't nothing. But it is within the reach of a huge number of people and is, in fact, far less than most of them would expect.

What makes that number less daunting is where the funds typically come from, according to Kauffman's research. More than a third—34.9 percent, to be exact—came from bank loans. Personal funds came second. As you can see from the table below, these two sources made up two-thirds of all funding, on average.

Where the Money Comes From

Major Categories	Amount	Share
Bank and Other Loans	$38,059	34.9%
Personal Savings	$32,658	30.0%
Friends and Family	$6,910	6.3%
Credit Cards	$6,756	6.2%
Angel Investors	$6,350	5.8%
Venture Capital	$4,804	4.4%
Government Related	$2,129	2.0%
Total	**$109,016**	**100%**

The way you might go about funding your business could be different, of course, since averages are only that—averages. Still, two intriguing things jump out from the research. One, despite the incredibly high interest rates credit card companies charge, people still use their cards as a source of funding. It is a bad idea. Two, as the study says, "you should not start planning your business around funding sources like VCs, angels, and government funding. They simply do not appear to be significant sources in most cases."

In fact, you might be able to get going with nothing more than your own personal resources and maybe a microloan—a short-term loan usually made to provide working capital and the other things necessary to get a new business going. You can get microloans from various sources, but let's take a look at how a U.S. Small Business Administration (SBA) microloan works, by way of example.

The SBA says its microloan program "provides small (up to $35,000) short-term loans for working capital or the purchase of inventory, supplies, furniture, fixtures, machinery and/or equipment." Now, that $35,000 figure doesn't seem like very much. But if the average business requires "just" $109,000 to get started, then that microloan could make up about a third of the money you need.

That $109,000 number is surprisingly small in part because of the way the best entrepreneurs go about building their businesses. It all goes back to the Act-Learn-Build-Repeat model we talked about in chapter 1. The best entrepreneurs don't swing for the fences, risking everything they have all at once, as the accepted myth would have you believe. They take a series of small steps toward their goals, learning as they go. With that approach, they only need enough funds to get to the next step. Good entrepreneurs are experts at controlling risk.

How Entrepreneurs Really Fund Their Businesses

"If you crack open most entrepreneurship textbooks, you'll find that they talk a lot about how entrepreneurs finance their businesses," begins a brilliant essay on the subject by Scott Shane, the A. Malachi Mixon III Professor of Entrepreneurial Studies at Case Western Reserve University. "Because these books are targeted at students in courses that focus on the creation of high-potential businesses, they spend a lot of time discussing venture capital, angel investing, and other sources of external equity capital. As a result, they don't describe how most entrepreneurs finance their businesses."

In reality, he says, there are four points to remember about start-up financing.

1. **Most business don't require a lot of start-up money.** Most entrepreneurs don't need much capital to get started, Shane notes. This is consistent with the Kauffman study's findings.

2. **Much of the money needed to finance new businesses comes from their founders.** "The most common source of that capital is the founder's own savings, with the majority of businesses only obtaining money from this source. As a result, more people finance their start-ups with their own money than get money from banks and friends and family members combined."

3. **External financing is more likely to be debt than equity.** "A study of young firms in Minnesota, Pennsylvania, and Wisconsin found that less than 10 percent of the firms had received an external equity investment, but half had borrowed money from an external source."

4. **Much of the borrowing is personally guaranteed.** Being incorporated protects your personal assets in case of bankruptcy. Lenders know that, however, and frequently make entrepreneurs sign for the loans personally, to make sure they can get their money back should the company fail.

What has worked for the best entrepreneurs will work for you, provided you understand—as we talked about in the previous chapter—your acceptable loss and never risk more than you can afford to lose. I doubt there is any reliable formula that can provide absolute security when venturing into the unknown—there is no action that guarantees a particular effort will succeed—but there is no doubt that applying the concept of affordable loss reduces the cost of failure (should there be one). But the approach does guarantee one thing: if you fail, you fail cheaply.

Protecting Your Pocketbook

Everything we have discussed in this chapter reinforces the point that entrepreneurs are not risk takers, they are calculated risk takers. I wish I had thought of that phrase, but I didn't. That defining characteristic of entrepreneurship is something that Leonard C. Green tells his students each semester at Babson College, which has been the number-one school for teaching entrepreneurship for as long as national magazines have been have been doing the rankings.

I mentioned Green earlier, when I talked about innovation. He is worth returning to here because of his track record in starting and funding successful ventures such as SoBe beverages and Blue Buffalo pet food.

> No one wants to fail. But if you are going to fail (and some things simply will not work out), you want to fail quickly and cheaply. That way you live to fight another day.

When Green says entrepreneurs are *calculated* risk takers, he speaks from experience. And he is happy to explain the distinction. "The difference between risk takers and calculated risk takers is the difference between failure and success," he says.

Risk takers bet everything on one roll of the dice. If they fail, they fail spectacularly and in such a way that they *don't* live to fight another day. They literally go out in a blaze of attempted glory.

But that *is not* what the best entrepreneurs do. "They only take small steps toward their goals, so they are not out much should they stumble, and before they take that small step, they figure out a way to minimize that tiny investment even further," Green explains. "They ask 'How can I take this step more cheaply (and/ or by using someone else's money); how can I do it faster (so I don't have to invest as much time) and how can I do it better than I had initially planned?'"

That, it seems to me, means they are as far from risk takers as they can be. Risk takers are *not* successful, as a rule. And the reason for that is simple, says Green: they leave too much to chance. And leaving things to chance can be very expensive.

Here's an example of minimizing expenses. Say you want to open a consumer electronics store. You could research the market forever, spend months putting together the perfect team, and take a lot of time gathering investors who can come up with the $2 million or so that it is going to take to get underway with a fully stocked store. And, eventually, you will open the doors to Easy Listening (and Viewing).

Or, on the very day you think of opening the store, you can start asking potential customers what they think of your idea. ("Hey, if I open a high-end consumer electronics place on Main Street, do you think you would give us a try?")

You learn from that small step. People might tell you there are an awful lot of consumer electronic stores around—including a fabulous stereo shop near your planned location that has existed since the days when Bing Crosby was recording 78s, and they are not sure that section of town needs another place to buy audio and stereo equipment.

At that point you could simply give up, or you could head in another direction. "Everyone told me there is probably not a market for another consumer electronics store, but people were intrigued by the idea of a 'concierge consumer electronics service' where they could go to a single source to find out not only what they should buy but where to buy it. Hmmmm."

Either way, you learned quickly. And even if you "failed"—that is, you decided not to open either the consumer electronics store or the concierge service—you did so quickly and at little cost. That means you have the resources to try again—something that the person who raised (and wasted) that $2 million might not be able to say.

Cost Savings

We have talked about how entrepreneurs are calculated risk takers, and those calculations extend to the way they spend every bit of their money. They are prudent businesspeople. And because they are, they don't spend money needlessly.

It is not the purpose of this book to outline every conceivable cost-saving measure that any business in general, or any entrepreneurial one in particular, might take. However, there are three particular—and not instantly intuitive—approaches that entrepreneurs use to get maximum return from their business, and it is worth spending a bit of time on each.

1. **Successful entrepreneurs are relentless in killing off underperforming products and services.** Everyone handles this differently. But the consensus seems to be to get rid of the bottom 10 percent of your product line each year. You want to be constantly introducing new things and eliminating the poorest performers, freeing up both resources and shelf space for new ones.

2. **They are remarkably respectful of their customers and employees.** The best leaders understand that

employees spend an inordinate amount of time watching what the boss does. And what I came to see, after talking to countless leaders and their employees, is that a boss's behavior is just as important as what she says.

Here's an example. There is a Southern car dealer who dominates his market. Not only is he number one, he has the same market share as the next four car dealers combined in the metro area where he competes. He is the third generation to lead the company and is invariably described as a "perfect Southern gentleman" when the business press profiles him. And I can vouch for the description. In fact, employees at his dealerships have only heard him raise his voice once in all the years he worked there. I happened to be there that day.

Some background is needed to explain what happened. Car dealership lots are congested and busy places. Not only are there a lot of cars, trucks, and vans but a great number of them are constantly in motion as they are rotated to the showroom, brought around for customers to see, or taken in for service. Not surprisingly, a lot of fender benders—and sometimes worse—occur in and around the showroom. At dealerships, that is not a big deal. Most own body shops, after all.

But common sense and respect for the customer demands that the dealer tell people when a car gets dinged up if it is one the customer is interested in (or worse, one he'd brought in for service).

Well, one day when I was visiting with the dealer, a top-of-line model that someone had just bought was damaged—a corner of the back bumper got mangled—while employees were preparing it for delivery to the customer. Repairs were made well before the customer showed up. The customer drove off the lot happy—never knowing what had happened. No one told him, and the car had been repaired to "like new" condition.

When the car dealer found out what happened he went what can only be described as ballistic. He gathered every employee who wasn't with a customer—and he has several hundred working for him—behind the showroom, explained what had happened, and literally yelled—using language most of them didn't know he knew—about how this was **not** how his company did business.

He explained that every customer was to be informed **any** time his car was damaged, no matter how minor the scratch. If the customer thought the repair was sufficient, fine. But if he wanted a credit or a different car—if he was buying a new one—then the employees were going to make him happy. That was ten years ago, and the incident has not been repeated since.

So, you have to believe the boss's behavior is important. The behavior that always resonated most with me was when the boss said thank you. Why is saying "thank you" important (besides the fact that it is good manners)? Every study I have seen about worker retention says that salary is consistently listed fourth, fifth, or sixth when people are asked why they stay at their job. Far more important is the fact that people like their jobs.

What makes people like their jobs? "I have a good boss," is always at the top of the list when the answers are compiled. And one of the reasons people give for liking that boss is that she says "thank you" when they do a good job.

Sure, you should pay good employees more. But you may not have to be at the top of the pay scale in your industry if you simply say "thank you" when appropriate. People want praise and recognition as well as a decent paycheck. Saying thank you is one of the best ways to provide the first two (and you cut your operating expenses in the process).

3. **Successful entrepreneurs make sure employees are not only adding value but are not hurting the organization.** When I say "hurting the organization," people always jump to embezzlement (or, on a milder note, stealing something like office supplies), but that is not what I am talking about. Nor am I being literal. Yes, of course, your employees are hurting the organization in the sense that they cost you money: you have to pay them, and that decreases profitablity. But that is not what is under discussion here. Rather, the most successful entrepreneurs make sure that their employees' interactions with potential customers are not turning those customers off and causing them to go elsewhere.

Here's a quick firsthand story to show what I am talking about. I needed a new dentist. A Google search coupled with consumer reviews identified one who looked promising. And he was okay, but I am not going back. My decision has nothing to do with him—it has to do with his office manager. Basically, she patronized me—which was annoying—and acted as if she was the dentist. "Oh, I don't think we will be able to reattach that," she said when I walked in for my appointment and handed her the crown I had managed to save. (The dentist could and did.) While I was seated in the dental chair waiting, she came by to explain what "probably will have to be done." (She was wrong on both the details and the timing.) And at a subsequent point she decided on her own that they should do a full set of x-rays to have on file when I came back, saying, "That's what the Dr. X is going recommend, so we might as well get started." I declined. By that point, I was pretty sure I wasn't coming back.

I suppose you could look on her actions as benign or rationalize that she was trying to lessen my anxiety by letting me know what to expect (she couldn't know that anyone who spends as much time as I do at the dentist's office is never anxious) or...her motivation doesn't matter. What matters are actions, and they annoyed me to the point where I am not going back. The dentist doesn't know this, since as far as I can tell he is not keeping a close eye on her, but the office manager cost her employer a lot of future income.

I have rotten teeth.

A Banker's "No" Could Tell You Something

I don't like bankers. Someday, over an adult beverage of your choice, I will explain the horror story that resulted when my wife and I tried to refinance our mortgage, and maybe in return you can explain why I am personally liable for my wife's business loan, though her company pledged four times the amount it borrowed as collateral and has a twenty-five-year history of performing well, has never come close to missing a loan payment, and is one of the most profitable firms in her industry.

My fondest goal in life is to be banker free. All that said, I think bankers can perform a useful function in the financing of your business. Yes, of course they can provide money. (And, as we saw from the Kauffman study, loans account for about 35 percent of the average start-up's funding.) But they can do more than that.

Bankers are skeptical. And while many entrepreneurs hate to admit it, bankers often do have some pretty valuable experience to offer. They can spot some of the pitfalls you may encounter as you go about building your business. They can tide you over the rough spots in the developmental phase. And, most important, they're there as devil's advocates when you're planning your next move.

That is why it's a useful exercise to put your proposed corporate strategy before these seasoned skeptics. You might not buy their conclusions. You may privately sneer at their apparent greed. You may bridle at their seemingly endless doubting questions. But never forget that, as an entrepreneur, you are naturally biased toward optimism and a belief you can overcome most hurdles. A little tempering of that with the cold water of bankers' bad experiences with companies very much like yours could prove constructive.

Very few businesspeople—small, corporate, or entrepreneurial—have the crucial ability to assess coldly and disinterestedly their true strengths and weaknesses. So look upon bankers as commercial psychiatrists of a sort. It won't make you like them more, but you may grow to appreciate their function.

You Don't Need to Spend Money to Make Money

People always look at me strangely when I say this, but an entrepreneur searching for a role model shouldn't look to Ray Kroc, who spotted the potential in the McDonald brothers' hamburger stand, or to Henry Ford. People who want to be more entrepreneurial, either to grow their own business or the company they work for, should look instead at that antithesis of individuality—the International Business Machine Corporation (IBM), at least when it comes to ways to minimize costs. Specifically, you should look at the way IBM created its personal computer. The company moved tens of millions of them before deciding to sell most of the division, for nearly $2 billion, to Lenovo in 2012.

As everyone knows, IBM didn't invent the personal computer. The prototype for the industry, the Altair, developed by a company called MITS, appeared in the mid-1970s. Apple Computer revolutionized the marketplace with the Apple II a little later, and by the time IBM decided to enter the market, there were already dozens of small firms making personal computers.

But as we have seen, entrepreneurship doesn't have to—and probably shouldn't—arise from new ideas, and clearly the IBM PC was nothing new. What IBM did when it decided to go into the personal computer business in 1980 was similar to what you probably do every Saturday morning. It went shopping.

If you took the PC apart, you'd find dozens of separate components. Few were made by IBM. The company simply scoured the country, buying disk drives from Tandon in California and software from Microsoft in Washington state, and so forth. "Anybody could have done what we did," an IBM spokesman told me candidly. "Part of the reason we went this route was speed. We wanted to enter the marketplace in a hurry, and it was quicker to buy off the shelf than for us to make it. The other reason was there was no compelling reason for us to do it ourselves. There were good components out there."

Think about that for a minute. Here is one of the most successful companies in American history saying, in essence, it didn't have to reinvent the wheel. There were good parts already out there; all the company had to do was put them together: *"We didn't have to do everything ourselves."* Put that way, the statement looks so obvious as to be absurd. Yet if you study the thousands of small companies that fail each year, you'll find there is at least one common thread: they spent money needlessly.

If you are going to be in business, you have to produce a

product, but that doesn't mean you have to manufacture it. Your product will have to be packaged somewhere, but you don't have to be the one doing the packaging.

Simply put, you *don't* have to spend money to make money. In fact, you shouldn't. That is something you want to impress upon your team as well.

Building a team is the subject of our next chapter.

Takeaways for Entrepreneurs and the Rest of Us

1. You are going to need substantially less money than you think to get underway, if you do things correctly.

2. Spending less allows you to experiment more, because you have the resources to do it.

3. To keep spending even lower, buy off-the-shelf components when you can.

CHAPTER 7

Building the Team

Getting a money-making idea is one thing. Making money from it is quite another. As we have seen, the hard part of starting a company is not coming up with a blockbuster idea—your concept doesn't have to be terrific. *Implementing* the idea is where both entrepreneurs and companies looking to be more entrepreneurial often stumble on the road to success.

That puzzled me for a long time. Why do many entrepreneurs have problems dealing with growth? About half of the companies that pass the financial screens to qualify as one of *Forbes*'s best small companies in America one year will fail to repeat the next. Why?

It turns out that dealing with growth hurdles almost always requires the entrepreneur to think in ways that are the *exact opposite* of what initially made him a success. Why this is so becomes clear if you trace the route that all entrepreneurs take, no matter where they work.

In the beginning, there is the idea that solves a market need. It comes from the entrepreneur. He thought of it and only he, at first, understands it completely. From there, the entrepreneur works to build a company. Initially, he makes all the decisions himself and does almost all the work, from product design to bookkeeping, alone. Most often, he doesn't have any choice. There is simply no money to pay anyone else.

However, that very self-reliance, which is vital to getting the company up and running quickly, can keep it from growing later. Independence to the point of orneriness is fine when a company is small. There is no bureaucracy to keep it from moving quickly to exploit openings in the marketplace.

But the desire for complete control is a major problem because it limits growth. Quite simply, an entrepreneur can't keep doing everything herself—and she shouldn't. But that is a difficult lesson to learn, and it is perhaps most evident when it comes to building a team. And that's a huge problem because creating a profitable business invariably involves hiring people to be part of your team.

Starting with Employee Number 1

Not surprisingly, the decision to begin adding staff is difficult. Most entrepreneurs I talked with tried to put off hiring someone for as long as possible, and their timing for pulling that trigger and hiring was remarkably similar in each case. The people I interviewed were, not surprisingly, an overachieving bunch who agreed that working at more than 100 percent of personal capacity is okay, until you wake up one day and decide that you can't do it any more. And once these entrepreneurs had hit their limit, they hired their first employee. But even then, they started small.

They often hired somcone half time, or even for a few hours a week. If that went well, they would go further. If it didn't go well, they stopped and evaluated. (You'll notice the process is extremely similar to the Act-Learn-Build-Repeat model we have talked about throughout.)

The successful entrepreneurs I spoke with made two other points that help form the foundation for this chapter. First, offshoring—the practice of shipping work overseas to places where labor costs are less—works better in theory than practice; I didn't talk to a single entrepreneur who said she had a good experience with it.

Second, and this was my favorite, whenever possible they tried to hire contract workers—people who are paid for accomplishing specific agreed-upon tasks—instead of full-time employees. Even if they paid more on an hourly basis, the arrangement worked out to be less expensive overall because they were only paying for the work they received.

Looking in the Mirror

Intriguingly, the biggest problem in creating the right team centered around the entrepreneurs themselves. Pierre Omidyar, the founder of eBay, in an interview he did with *Inc.*, explained both the problem and the solution perfectly: "When I first started working as a software engineer, I had really high standards, and I often felt other people weren't meeting them. But over time, I realized that even if others on the team weren't doing everything as perfectly as I wanted them to, if they got to 80 percent of the way there then that was awesome."

Why? "Because there were five of them," Omidyar said, "and five times 80 percent is much larger than 100 percent of me. That led me into this idea of leveraging other people."

Team Building Is So Very Hard to Do

Academics and others who have never run a company go on at seemingly endless length about how working through others is the most logical thing in the world and anyone who doesn't do it, or who doesn't do it well, is a dolt. The people who run companies know better. They have learned firsthand just how hard working with and through others can be. Managing even one person is difficult. (Ask anyone who has hired an assistant for the first time.) So, in the course of reporting this book, I was not surprised to find many entrepreneurs who were running multimillion-dollar businesses and were still doing tasks that could be easily handled by someone else.

Eventually, the most successful entrepreneurs learn that even if employees don't do everything as well as they do, if those employees come close they will—as Omidyar said—have substantially exceeded what the entrepreneur could do on her own.

That said, there are two things the entrepreneurs I talked with said you need to do before hiring anyone. Yes, you probably need a Ms. Inside to your Mr. Outside. Or a finance whiz. Or maybe an energetic go-getter who . . . . Before you add anyone, they suggest that you first take a good look in the mirror. Do this not only at the beginning, but every step of the way; in building a strong team you want someone who has skills that complement your own.

This is the point we made in chapter 4 when we said you want to build up your strengths and hire someone to offset your weaknesses, instead of spending time that could be better used elsewhere trying to offset them yourself.

Owning up to your own shortcomings can be difficult, and it can be tough to overcome the natural tendency to want to work on your weaknesses. But that is exactly what you need to do.

That brings us to the second thing you want to do. In addition to those complementary skills, you need to look at the other resources the people you hire or partner with can bring to the table. In an ongoing enterprise, a needed resource could be a greater understanding of the markets you are trying to serve. In a start-up, it could be money or contacts. The vast majority of successful entrepreneurs I talked to brought others into the process early on, hiring those who had complementary skills and a lot to bring to the party. This is, of course, contrary to the accepted myths about how the best entrepreneurs do business. (See our discussion in chapter 2.)

Don't Sell People on Joining You: Enroll Them

A large pool of people who can help make your vision a reality is a wonderful resource. But how do you go about building your team? Your first inclination will be to try to sell them on what a wonderful idea you have and how exciting the future is going to be. After that, you might want to talk about their roles, salaries, stock options, and the like, all as part of your sales process.

Honest selling is a noble profession. Great salespeople can make your life easier when you are looking to buy. But while a great salesperson wants you to be happy, her ultimate focus is in getting you to do what she wants: to buy her goods or services. Her goal is to make the sale that benefits her. That isn't a great foundation on which to build a team.

Let me suggest a different way of going about it. Instead of selling potential employees, try to get them to enlist or enroll. When someone enrolls it is because you have inspired him to act in favor of what *he* wants to do. That person becomes part of your efforts because he is excited by your dream and wants to join you in making it a reality. The essence of enrollment is that your efforts become his efforts as well.

Enrollment is about offering people the chance to do something they want to do (in this case, become part of your effort). You don't convince them. They truly convince themselves. It's a voluntary, personal commitment on their parts, and because it is, the commitment runs deeper.

Getting that enrollment to happen is a pretty straightforward process.

Step 1: Be enrolled yourself. You can't expect to gain the commitment of others if you're not committed yourself. You must *want* to make your idea a reality. Starting anything new is hard enough if you are committed. Others sense when you are not enrolled. They can tell you are not excited about the idea or truly committed to making it happen. And if they get that feeling, they are bound to ask: "If he is not really into it, why should I be?"

If you try to enroll someone when you are not truly enrolled yourself, you'll end up selling, and you probably won't even do a very good job of it.

Step 2: Be honest. It really is the best policy. You are truly committed to your idea. Now you want to get people to come along. What's the next step?

You talk to potential hires about what you want to do, and you are genuine and transparent. You give them a complete picture. Not only do you tell them the positives and negatives, to the extent you know them, you also tell them why your idea is so important to you. If it is because you want to make a lot of money, tell them. If it really is all about making a small part of the world a better place, say that. Remember, one of the results of enrolling people is that you form a lasting relationship. You are putting in all this effort because you want first and foremost an authentic foundation on which you can build trust and joint action. You can only build this kind of meaningful relationship if you are being forthright.

People enroll with you, perhaps even more than with your vision. That's why you tell the complete truth. After you do, they will either join you or they won't. That is just the way it goes. There's nothing you can do to "get some-one to enroll." When you try, you'll invariably become manipulative and start selling your vision. The person you are trying to sell will see right through it. People can immediately sniff out when you are trying to get them to do something, even if it is in their best interest. There is no reason to go down this road when what you are looking for is genuine commitment to your cause. People either want to enroll or they don't.

People will only enroll when what you have resonates within *them*. The deeper the connection between what you are talking about and what is important to them, the more likely they are to put their shoulder to your wheel along-side you. And, fortunately, that happens fairly frequently. When it does, you end up discussing what is important to both of you. At that point, your vision becomes even clearer to you and actually changes, even if only a bit, to become *our vision*.

Step 3: Offer action. An integral part of the enrollment process is immediately offering the person who wants to join you some real work to do, even if it is a part-time job. When that action occurs, you know enrollment has taken place.

When Do You Transition?

As small companies grow, the founder can no longer do everything herself. Many refuse to delegate, and their companies stop grow-ing. Their companies never become any bigger than one person can handle. But even for companies that recognize the problem, the transition from individual control to broad-based management is difficult and scary. Turning over (even part of) what you created to someone else is a huge psychological move.

When do you take that step? The answer, perhaps surprisingly, is immediately upon creation, according to the majority of the entrepreneurs I talked to. Even when the start-up is small enough for one person to do everything, one person should not be doing it all. Why? The answers run the gamut from practicality to human nature.

What strikes me, after talking to several hundred chief executives of emerging growth companies, is how few are comfortable and good at creating new ideas and also managing organizations. Maybe one in ten perform well in both roles. Some don't have the temperament—not only do they not suffer fools gladly, they are not crazy about people who are as bright as they are. They are not the kind of people you want handling personnel. Other entrepreneurs couldn't organize a pickup softball game, let alone a company, if their lives depended on it. And indeed, their companies' lives do depend on it.

But the argument for early delegation of power goes beyond the entrepreneur's ability to shuffle papers and mange people. It goes to the heart of effective management in an emerging company. As their companies grow quickly, entrepreneurs find they are spending an increasing amount of time dealing with *personal* personnel crises—like an employee needs a $20,000 advance on his salary or he will lose his house. Maybe the entrepreneur can deal with these kinds of problems with dispatch and maybe he can't. But the fact is, he shouldn't have to.

What entrepreneurs are good at, by definition, is figuring out ways to compete differently: finding holes in the marketplace and ways to exploit them. That's what got them into business, not the ability to thrive within a large organization. Indeed, most of these people left large organizations because they didn't like the environment or could not function effectively within it. If they couldn't cope with a large organization when they worked for one, how are they going to build and run one effectively? The vast majority of them won't.

Recognizing that reality, they should make plans early in their companies' lives to deal with that fact. How? Relatively simple tasks should be delegated as soon as the company starts to grow. It doesn't have to be anything elaborate at first. Administrative assistants can fill out insurance forms; the person who stocks the shelves can order supplies. Ideally, those people can handle increased responsibilities as the company expands. To ensure that happens, overqualified people should be hired for each new position as the company experiences rapid growth. The temptation is to hire cheap. That's wrong, because you'll only get what you pay for.

There is also a temptation to deal with pending organizational problems by saying, "We will cross that bridge when we come to it." That's wrong, too. The odds are, by the time you get to the bridge it will be too late.

Emerging companies grow quickly. In addition to being able to respond to a changing market, the entrepreneur must be able to deal with the organization that will be emerging within his company as it experiences rapid growth. Anticipating internal personnel and administrative problems is vital if the external business plan is to have any chance of success. The takeaway? Delegate before you have to.

Empower Your People

Let's expand on that last point about delegating. Given how hard it is to create anything, and how much passion is required to overcome the inevitable obstacles you will face, the last thing you want to do is get in your own way. But I guarantee you will be tempted to.

Let me explain. Invariably, people who start companies assign themselves the position of CEO. That's understandable, of course: the company is their idea. But there are many different ways of being a CEO, and unfortunately a majority of people gravitate toward the old command-and-control model, in which the boss's fingerprints can be found on everything.

Can that work? Sure. But there are four problems.

1. The business can never grow bigger than one person (you, the CEO) can manage effectively.
2. The company can't move very quickly. Because everything has to flow through you, you create a bottleneck. People have to wait for you to sign off before they can move ahead. (There is typically a line outside your office from morning to night as a result.)
3. You won't get the best ideas out of your people. Once they understand that the company is set up so that everything revolves around you, your employees will not take the time to develop their best ideas. "Why should I?" they ask. "He is just going to do what he wants anyway."
4. It's exhausting.

A far better approach is to let employees make as many decisions as they can, allowing them to implement the decisions as well. Every time I say this, people ask me if I am worried about employees making mistakes. My answer? "Not really."

For one thing, everyone makes mistakes. Employees made mistakes before they were empowered, and it would be silly to believe they wouldn't make any once they were. But an intriguing thing happens when you start letting people make their own decisions. Invariably, the number of mistakes goes down. When employees feel you are going to make the final decision anyway, they don't always think through what they are doing. Once the decision is theirs, they tend to be not only more creative but more careful.

Unfortunately, you are going to make mistakes in hiring people. It comes with the territory. However, you can reduce problems by hiring people more qualified than you initially need them to be. At first they may not have enough to do, but as the company grows they will be able to take on more responsibility. This way, you will have on hand the people you need as your company takes off. You won't have to waste time searching for them.

Do you give your employees carte blanche? No. Do you supervise them (rather than micromanage them)? Yes. You want to make sure they are not doing anything to hurt the company. And you reserve the right to have the final say when it comes to decisions. But I guarantee you that, after a while, you are going to use your veto power less and less. It's like anything else, the more practice employees get at making decisions, the better decisions they will make.

If the idea still makes you nervous, start small. Put a dollar limit on the decisions: "If the decision involves less than $500, you don't need approval." Raise that limit over time, if things are going well.

Will empowering employees work for you? I truly believe it will, if you can wrap your mind around giving up control. There are three things to remember with this strategy. First, as we discussed before, you are going to have to pay to get the kind of people you need. You really do get what you pay for.

Second, the people you hire initially may not be the best ones to run your company five or ten years in. Your company will change, and so will your management needs. While it is a painful realization, be prepared to bring in new—and even higher-priced—help. And at some point, earlier in the process than you will care to admit, you will have to start planning for an orderly management succession. If you are planning on dying with your boots on, your company might too.

Finally, if you delegate and empower, you will be free to do the things you like and think about where you want to take the company. You don't have time to think if you are constantly putting out fires.

Teammates Can Come from Outside the Enterprise

Once she is off and running, almost every successful entrepreneur bumps into serious, unexpected problems. Even the best business plan won't anticipate everything because the marketplace keeps changing. Entrepreneurs who vault the make-or-break hurdles in this third phase (after coming up with the idea and marketing it successfully) of the start-up's life are those who use their fledgling staffs and limited resources effectively.

The best way to do that is to recognize from the very beginning that neither you nor your company should try to do everything. Those who attempt to go it alone—either in management or manufacturing—rarely succeed for long.

We explored above the point about why you should delegate internally. Now let's talk about why delegating is a good thing for your organization as well. By subcontracting wherever possible, you not only free up capital, you don't waste valuable time learning another business. That is time that can be used figuring out how to compete differently.

Don't worry that farming out work will cost more. By playing one contractor off another, you are guaranteed to receive a price almost as low as if you did it yourself. Just as you should concentrate on what you do best and delegate other tasks to someone who is better at them, your company should take the same approach. Have your firm concentrate on its strengths and outsource the rest.

Now, does this advice fly in the face of the experience the best entrepreneurs have with off-shoring, that is sending work overseas? No, for two reasons. The kind of outsourcing I am talking about here involves having the work done by a domestic corporation. That company may or may not send the work overseas, but you will be dealing with someone within the United States, so you won't have to deal with all the logistical headaches that come with dealing with organizations half a world away.

Second, I am talking about paring down your company to what it does best—marketing, distribution, whatever—and letting recognized experts handle everything else for you.

Business 101: Study the Competition

When most people read the words in that headline, they instantly jump to analyzing their competitors to see what they are doing wrong and what opportunities they are missing. And that is, indeed, an extremely important thing to do. Finding niches that others have overlooked or are underserving may lead to new opportunities for you. That creates a twofold win. Not only are you helped, but the competition is hurt.

But when you are studying the people and organizations you are up against, don't forget to look at what the competition is doing right. For one thing, they had to be doing something right to get into business. People don't start companies on a whim. For another, they must be doing at least one thing right if they are still in business. They cannot be complete dolts.

But there are more reasons than the fact of their survival that you should study them. And that is especially true when it comes to how they go about building their team. Are their employees better than yours? Why? Is it training? The competition's hiring process? How those employees are supervised? Motivated? Compensated? Is the competition doing interesting things with their benefits programs or the way they promote? What you are trying to discover is what the competition does right that you could do as well.

Don't Hurt the Team

It is hard to pick up a newspaper without reading about some company paying millions—or, in some cases, billions—to settle charges of misbehavior (JPMorgan Chase seems determined to retire with the title). And it is not just corporations making the front page with their bad behavior. If it weren't for the silly (or stupid or criminal) actions of politicians and celebrities, I am not sure your daily paper would have enough news to print.

Here's why I am bringing this up. When you are in doubt about what to do, it would be lovely to think you will automatically do the right thing. The problem with that is threefold:

1. **Right and wrong are sometimes a bit squishy.** While there are some absolutes (Murder is bad, funding an orphanage? Good), things are not always that cut and dried. (Can you deduct a long boozy dinner with a former boss who is no longer in a position to do you any good? Should you?)

2. **Sometimes right and wrong is not a matter of morality at all.** You are the forty-five-year-old CEO of a small company and you are traveling to the opposite coast for a meeting. Should you be wearing your most comfortable sweatpants on what amounts to a business commuter flight?

3. **It sometimes seems right and wrong have an industry context.** Should you get people to take the absolute largest mortgage they qualify for, if you know that once the "introductory" rate expires they will be in financial trouble? How about charging 20 percent of

the purchase price for the "nontransferrable" lifetime warranty on a product you are selling to an eighty-five-year-old?

Things are not always clear when it comes to ethics. So, what standard should you use? In the words of Jiminy Cricket, you could always just let your conscience be your guide. But your sense of morality may not be the same as everyone else's (either good or bad).

Let me give you an alternative. When in doubt—and perhaps even when you are not in doubt—ask yourself, "Would I want what I am about to do to appear on the front page of tomorrow's newspaper?" You can rant and rave about reporters if you want or say the media tends to sensationalize everything. That's fine. But the fact is that the image you have of corporate wrongdoing and questionable behavior of politicians and celebrities comes from reading the news—in the paper or online—or from watching it on TV or listening to it on the radio. And the standards that were used in reporting on all those people are the same ones that will be applied to you.

Sure, odds are that you won't come to a reporter's attention, but:

1. I am sure that is what everyone who ends up being embarrassed by press reports said . . . before they became news.
2. You might.

That's something to keep in mind before you act.

Fire the Bottom 10 Percent?

Back when he was running GE, Jack Welch famously argued that leaders should fire the bottom 10 percent of their workforce each year, as part of an orderly continuous improvement process. Some entrepreneurs embrace the idea completely. They like the discipline it imposes. "It is one thing to say that you always want to be upgrading your staff, it is another to actually do it," one entrepreneur told me. "The 10 percent rule—and that is how we think of it, as a rule—forces us to constantly improve our staffing. Yes, of course, we work with underperformers. But the fact remains, we always get rid of the bottom 10 percent each year."

Other entrepreneurs said the approach was simply too draconian. They didn't want to be viewed as that kind of organization. They said they were committed to improving the performance of employees, and only when they were convinced good performance wasn't possible would they let someone go. Said one entrepreneur who heads a very successful—and profitable—consulting firm: "My personal feeling about the organizations that make it a hard-and-fast rule to fire people? They aren't doing a particularly good job in how they hire. We handle firings on a case-by-case basis. And if we ever got up to 10 percent, and we have never come close, we would totally overhaul the way we handle recruitment. Something would be terribly wrong."

The point of agreement here? You should always be trying to improve the quality of your employees. You don't have to have a hard-and-fast rule, such as fire the bottom 10 percent every year, but you do want to be reviewing your entire workforce once a year (at the very least), with an eye toward constantly improving it. That could mean helping existing employees get better. But it could also mean bringing in more talented people.

Diversity

You have probably used the following phrase yourself. It's said when you and a colleague, employee, or even a friend come up with a remarkably similar solution to a problem you are trying to solve.

After you have realized that you both basically came up with the same solutions, someone says: "Great minds think alike." And everyone smiles.

But maybe you shouldn't. Great minds thinking alike is often a problem as people go about building their companies. If you and the people around you see the world in exactly the same way, the ideas you are going to come up with are going to be remarkably similar as well. And that isn't good.

What we need today is as many *different* good ideas as possible, so we can pick the absolute best one. And that means we need different perspectives and different ways of approaching and solving market needs.

Agreeing that these different perspectives are necessary is difficult for many entrepreneurs. They are used to being the smartest person in the room. Who could possibly have better ideas than me, they ask. Well, a lot of people could. That is especially true if the collaborator has a different background in terms of employment, upbringing, where she lives, went to school, whatever. Someone with a dissimilar background will simply see things in a different way, and so her solutions are often radically different and (unfortunately for the entrepreneur's ego) better.

You don't want diversity for diversity's sake. It does you no good to surround yourself with people whose age, gender, and ethnicity are different from yours if you don't listen to them. But if you do, the ideas you generate as a group may very well be better. So, the next time you find yourself in a situation where the appropriate thing to say is "Great minds think alike," by all means say it. And then check that the minds you are calling on to solve problems are really different from yours.

You want the strongest team possible in order to come up with the best solutions and deal with the inevitable obstacles you will face. That is the subject of our next chapter.

Takeaways for Entrepreneurs and the Rest of Us

1. Hire before you have to. No one will ever doubt your work ethic. Still, for the good of the enterprise you are leading, bring people on board sooner rather than later.

2. Hire better than you have to. Don't cheap out. Add over-qualified people to your team, people who will be able to handle increasing amounts of responsibility.

3. Delegate before you have to. Distribute authority as far and as fast as you can. Everyone will benefit.

CHAPTER 8

How the Most Successful People Turn Obstacles into Assets

Clueless managers and the clichés they utter are always good for a laugh whether we are talking about movies (*Office Space),* television (anything from *Bewitched* to *The Office)* to plays (*How to Succeed in Business [Without Really Trying])* to comic strips (*Dilbert).* In a world of limited resources, the idea of "win–wins" doesn't happen often. "Giving 110 percent" is just, well, "fuzzy math." As for "We have to push the envelope," have you ever actually tried to push an envelope? It's a lot like "pushing string" or "herding cats." It ain't easy.

As a refugee from corporate America—once upon a time I was a middle-level manager for the largest division of a *Fortune 500* company—it's not surprising that I am not fond of these clichés (since I heard them constantly, and without irony, and every time I did my work life ended up being more difficult.)

However, there is one that I think is worth paying attention to: "There are no such things as problems, just opportunities." And it is especially true for entrepreneurs and people who would like their area of responsibility to be more entrepreneurial. Given competition—both global and local—capital restraints, and just the plain unexpected, when it comes to making progress in our business today, things rarely move in a straight line.

That means more problems—but more opportunities, if you view those challenges in a different way. **The key is to focus on your goal and not on the plan you initially drew up to get there.** If you do—and I think you must—your objective doesn't change. (You are still going to open that new market or introduce an additional product or service.) But you accept the fact that the way you get there may become different from the path you thought you were going to follow.

For those of us who were trained—as I was—in putting together five-year forecasts, three-year plans, and annual budgets, this is going to require thinking differently, something that is never a walk in the park. We are used to assuming the world is a predictable place but just skimming the headlines shows that it no longer is. However, we need to embrace the volatility and use it to our advantage.

To see how this new approach might work, we need to begin by taking a step back. In the world we grew up in, we were taught either to avoid the unexpected or to overcome it. It was all about efficiency. Optimizing. Achieving the objective quickly with as few deviations as possible. That's understandable. Before we began anything new we usually spent a lot of time trying to figure out what was going to happen (predicting), and once we got underway it was all about making that prediction a reality. Not surprisingly, people got upset when something unexpected appeared in their path; their reaction was to try to eliminate or overcome the deviation from the plan ASAP.

In today's world, however, the key to success is exploiting the contingencies and leveraging the uncertainty by treating unexpected events as opportunities to exercise control over the emerging situation. (We don't have any choice. Think of the last time you drew up a plan to accomplish something and it went off without a hitch. It's been a long while, hasn't it?)

Those who are successful in starting companies, or creating anything new for that matter, learn not only to work with the surprise factor but to take advantage of it.

Plan B Can Be Good, Too

Now, as I said, plan B can take some time to get used to. You need to accept that your fallback position could end up being more valuable than your original idea.

In most contingency plans, surprises are bad; the "what if?" scenarios are usually worst-case ones. But people who accept that the world is much more complex today do not tie themselves to any theorized or preconceived market, strategic universe, or fixed path for making their idea a reality. For them, problems are a potential resource rather than a disadvantage. These enterprising people often do something with the information and events that surprise and even frustrate them at first, treating the unexpected as a potential asset.

How do you get creative with a surprise? Well, if the surprise is a good one, you take full advantage of it. For example, you thought (or at least hoped) the world would love your new lawn care product. But you have been overwhelmed by demand. The logical thing to do is to ramp up production, add distributors (perhaps worldwide), and think about creating additional products not only for lawns, but for flowers, trees, and garden design applications as well.

If that surprise was a negative one—that is, your actions did not go as you thought they would and you encountered a problem or a setback—it is time to figure out a way of using that negative to your advantage. You read about this sort of thing all the time. 3M develops an adhesive that fails to consistently stick, and turns it into the basis of the Post-it Note. Minoxidil was originally developed to treat high blood pressure, but it turned out to be better at growing hair. You probably know it as Rogaine.

Problems = Advantage

Running headlong into a problem and then solving it can create a barrier to competition, or at least create a remarkable head start in the marketplace. Why? Because you acted and the competition didn't. As a result, you know something your competitors don't.

Isadore Sharp, founder of the upscale Four Seasons Hotels and Resorts chain, serves as a case in point. When he started out, he assumed that the only thing that would matter was putting his hotels in the best locations. The problem he ran into was that every other hotel chain had the same idea. That was a huge negative surprise. If you are doing what everyone else is, you don't have an advantage.

In solving that problem, Sharp stumbled on what turned out to be the Four Seasons' ultimate competitive advantage. In fact, he created two of them. Because he had so many hotels, he could offer the frequent traveler who was used to a high level of comfort one-stop shopping when it came to a stay in any of the world's major cities. If you wanted the best, you simply called the Four Seasons.

The other advantage, Sharp decided, would be his employees. What he understood was that the people who wanted luxury also expected superior service. They wanted their every need taken care of, and anticipated if possible. They were willing to pay for being taken care of. So Sharp made the decision to raise the hotels' level of service to the point where it matched everything else within the facilities—the décor, the food, and the surroundings.

Other luxury hotel brands eventually caught on. But the Four Seasons had a huge head start and remains committed to maintaining it by constantly improving. The result? Location was no longer the differentiator, since competitors could not only open in the same city but in some cases literally down the same block. The huge advantage now was the company's people and the level of service they could provide.

So, any negative surprise you encounter can ultimately become a barrier to competition, if you treat it as an asset, as Sharp did. He accepted that what he thought was going to be an advantage—location—wasn't. (Everyone else could build in the same place.) He took that fact ("we have terrific locations, but many other people do too") and asked what he could do with that fact. His conclusion: we can provide excellent service at these superior locations. That has given him a terrific edge in the marketplace.

Coming Full Circle

We began this chapter by talking about business clichés. Let's end this section of it the same way. The takeaway from what we have talked about so far is clear: if you get lemons—otherwise known as business problems/obstacles—do indeed make lemonade. What does that mean for you? Well, the next time you are confronted with something unexpected, something that you would normally see as a problem, tell yourself, "This is really good news," and then try to make it so by turning it into an advantage or using it as a springboard to something else.

> Always ask, "How can I turn this problem into an asset or opportunity?"

What you want to do is build up a new creative muscle, one that allows you to turn problems into profits. That means your default position should be that there is never a problem without a potential profitable/pleasant solution lurking somewhere. Work with the understanding that (1) not all surprises are bad, and (2) surprises, whether good or bad, can be used to create something new. This idea is central to the way we need to think going forward. The secret is to do something positive with those surprises. Indeed, it is what the most successful entrepreneurs do. They consider everything—including obstacles that the rest of us would consider to be problems—as a gift.

There are three reasons why entrepreneurs adopt this mind-set. First, you need to make reality your friend. You can wish, hope, plan, and dream but eventually you are going to find out what people do and don't like about your idea. Better to learn it as soon as possible, before you sink more resources into the idea, venture, or product line. You want to keep potential losses to a minimum, as we have said throughout. It is an integral part to the Act-Learn-Build-Repeat model.

Second, the market reaction could actually lead you to create a better product or service. You saw that with Sharp's repositioning of the Four Seasons. He thought his barrier to competition was going to be location, but it turned out to be his people.

Third, you are no longer dealing in the hypothetical. (I wonder what will happen if I open an upscale hotel in a major city.) You get evidence. True, the evidence may be not what you wanted. ("Hmm. Everyone just expects there to be extremely nice hotels in big cities. I am not getting any points for offering another luxury one.) You now know exactly what you are up against. ("I will need to find another way to compete. Maybe the way to go is with a smaller, extended-stay luxury hotel. We'll offer everything that the Four Seasons, Taj, and Raffles do, but provide only suites that contain a fully equipped kitchen and a washer and dryer.")

Turning problems into opportunities is what the best entreprenuers do all the time. People with a health concern (diabetes) start services to help those who are affected; Yvon Chouinard, an avid rock climber, couldn't find equipment he liked, so he created his own. You probably know him better as the founder of Patagonia, a company famous for its quality sports equipment and apparel. Bernie

Goldhirsh struggled for years trying to start a sailing magazine in the early 1970s. His problem? There were no resources for budding entrepreneurs to draw on—all the business magazines at that time were geared toward people who worked for large companies, so he had to learn his lessons the hard way. Goldhirsh started *Inc.* magazine to help people just like him. Some thirty-five years later the idea still resonates with entrepreneurs and would-be entrepreneurs.

The thing to remember is this: when faced with the unknown, effective people work with what they have at hand, whatever comes along. They use everything at their disposal. That is why they are grateful for surprises, obstacles, and even disappointments. It gives them more information and resources to draw upon.

D'Oh!

We all like confirmation that something we believe is correct. I got mine, for this chapter, from my favorite antihero, Homer Simpson of *The Simpsons*.

After realizing he has lived half his life and doesn't have much to show for it, Homer, in one of my favorite episodes, is inspired by Thomas Alva Edison and sets out to become an inventor.

Not surprisingly, given that this is Homer, most of his inventions—a horn that sounds every three seconds when everything is perfectly okay, a musket that women have to aim at their face to apply makeup—are profoundly lame. Silly, but lame. But in the midst of creating these dumb ideas, Homer inadvertently comes up with a good one.

While he was pondering his next invention, Homer would lean back in his chair...and promptly fall over. This happens repeatedly. To solve the problem he creates a chair with two hinged legs on the back, making it impossible to tip over backward. Voilà! A new invention is born.

If Homer Simpson can turn a problem into an innovative solution, so can you.

Why Are We Talking So Much About Obstacles?

I talk about obstacles in depth because, well, things will go wrong. This idea is so obvious, I almost didn't include it. I have argued that the best way to deal with uncertainty is to:

- Take a small step toward what you want.
- Learn from taking that small step.
- Build that learning into the next small step you take.
- Learn from that one (and so on).

At the very heart of the Act-Learn-Build-Repeat model is the fact that you are going to make what are, by any objective measure, mistakes. You thought people would be clamoring for your Portuguese/Brazilian/Cubano fusion restaurant fare. They weren't. You were absolutely convinced that your blog on the inner workings of the investment banking industry would be hot...and the response never warmed beyond room temperature. You only got a thousand readers.

Throughout, I have said these less-than-wonderful responses are a good thing. You learned something, and that new understanding could take you in another direction. You might offer ethnic takeout dinners instead of opening a sit-down restaurant or, in an effort to make your blog profitable, decide to charge each of your thousand readers, who desperately need the information you provide, $5,000 annually to find out what only you know—and all of a sudden you have a $5 million business. So, I have argued, that initial failure is actually something you should embrace. And you should.

But at the moment when people tell you they don't like your restaurant or blog idea in their original forms, the news is devastating. No one likes bad news, and your first response is not likely to be, "Oh, good, I've learned something that I can apply next time," but rather, "Why did I waste all that time, money, and effort? How stupid could I be?" Unhappiness and depression—at least for a time—invariably follow.

I understand about mistakes. I've been there. (Someday I will tell you all about the companies I tried to start with friends, companies that no one was interested in, and book ideas that publishers yawned at.) So I know how demoralizing that initial rejection can be.

Nobody likes to fail. Nobody likes to hear "No" or "That's a dumb idea." Nobody likes to put a lot of effort into something she believes in only to be rebuffed. But, it is part of the process, unfortunately. Knowing that helps (at least in the long term).

Someone I know who sells extremely high-end products (and receives a wonderful commission for each one sold) did the math one day and realized that, on average, for every one hundred people he pitched only five said yes. So, he had a one in twenty success rate. As a result of that realization, he would say to himself something like, "Now I only have to approach nineteen (or eighteen or seventeen) more people to make a sale," every time he got turned down, instead of feeling demoralized by the rejection.

I try to keep that thought in mind when people turn me down, and I remember these two thoughts as well:

- Having people say no is part of the process (darn it).
- This is the reason I make small bets (so the losses are not so painful).

It helps. A bit.

Mind-Set

Dealing with setbacks can be difficult. And yet it is part of being an entrepreneur. When I served on a grand jury recently, I met someone with exactly the mind-set you need to have. Our foreperson was an entrepreneur in her mid-forties and was always well dressed. One day she arrived a bit late and her hair—which I suddenly realized was an expensive wig—was slightly mussed.

As one of the other women on the jury helped her fix it, our foreperson thanked her and said to the group, "I am so sorry I was late. Chemo went longer and was a bit tougher than usual." We started to make consoling noises—she had never told us or the judge (who would have excused her from serving) that she was sick—but she cut us off. "Thank you," she said. "But we all have something. Let's get to work."

There is absolutely no doubt in my mind that this woman will continue to have an extremely successful career once her treatment is finished. And that brings us to a related point.

Never Complain

Every successful person is unique. How could it be otherwise? But one of the things all have in common is this: they don't whine.

I noticed early on that the most successful people rarely (or never) talked about the difficulties that they had to overcome. For the longest time I thought it was modesty, but eventually I realized they didn't talk about it because they didn't think there was anything to talk about. They had a problem or a series of them. They took their problems as a given and worked hard to play the best hand they could with the cards they were dealt. If the problem was caused by something they had done, they took great pains not to do it again. But if it was just a matter of fate, they accepted it and started working on a way to overcome it. They took the attitude that there is nothing to be gained by complaining—and they are absolutely correct.

As former Notre Dame coach Lou Holtz once said: "Never tell people your problems. Ninety percent of them won't care and the rest will be glad you have them."

Yes, it is a funny line. It is also true.

Digging Deeper

There is a school of thought that says entrepreneurs—and other successful people—achieve their success because of the problems they face. They work to overcome the problems in such a way that leads to new opportunities, opportunities they would not have had except for the obstacles.

I think that is too pat an answer. Sure, it happens sometimes, but I think that saying the obstacle *caused* the success is a stretch in most cases. I am not willing to go that far (although I know there are motivational speakers who make a very nice living telling people like me our position is wrong). I think smart, driven people remain smart, driven people, no matter what the circumstances. Whatever your position on this, we can all agree that successful people don't let an obstacle remain an obstacle for long. They face it head on and work to overcome it.

Here's where I come out on this. A friend told me the following is Buddhist wisdom. I don't know if he is right, but I know the thought is: "In life, pain is mandatory. Suffering is optional." In other words, don't whine. Just get the job done.

Don't Get in Your Own Way

I am a big believer in ego, with one huge caveat. I will get to the exception in a minute, but I really do believe in the importance of ego in just about all spheres of life—and in business, particularly entrepreneurial business, a strong ego is an underrated asset. It is ego that allows you to get over the scary hump of starting something new. It is ego that convinces you that you can overcome whatever obstacles crop up. And it is ego that drives you to fill the market need and satisfy customers.

So, there is no doubt that ego is important. But...and it is a huge but: ego can also lead you to assume that your competition is not as good as it actually is, and that is a recipe for disaster. It is easy to understand how you might underestimate the people or companies you are up against. For one thing, you have thought of a new idea that makes you and your company special. The ability to identify and fill a market need is not unique, but it is rare. And you are right to be proud of yourself for having that ability.

For another, it is simply natural for you to want to overestimate how hard it would be for someone to replicate what you have. But while it's natural, the tendency flies in the face of reality. The universe is filled with people who are willing to work as hard as you do. (Not everyone does, but all it takes is one competitor to put a serious dent in what you have.)

And not only can they move as fast as you do but, since you have paved the way, they may be able to move a touch faster than you did when you started. You have shown them where both the obstacles and dead ends are. Don't underestimate them. Assume they are good, because they probably are, and then use their strengths against them.

How? Well, the first thing to do is figure out their greatest strength. It may not be obvious on the surface. Let's take Home Depot and Lowe's as examples. You might be tempted to say their greatest strength is low prices, but that's not it. Their prices are fine, but they are really nothing to write home about, even during sales. Their real advantage is inventory. Walk into one of those huge stores—they have literally several acres of selling space under one roof—and it is hard to imagine that they wouldn't have every home improvement item a customer might need.

So, how do you compete if you don't have the buying power of a big box store? That's simple. You recognize that their very size can be off-putting. It can take forever to find something or to stumble upon someone who can point you to the right aisle if you can't.

You could compete by curating the home improvement product line. You might carry only three SKUs of any product—a good, better, and best version—and/or offer better service. Suddenly, the huge size of the competition is less appealing. You have turned their very strength against them.

Don't Create an Obstacle Before You Have To

I have written a lot about failure in this book. I am in favor of it. Not the kind of failure where you bet everything on one roll of the dice and lose. That kind of failure is devastating because you have used up all your resources and you don't get to try again.

No, the kind of failure I am talking about is when you take a small step toward your goal and find it doesn't work. That kind of failure is far from fatal, and in fact can be helpful if you learn from it and put that learning to use with the next small step you take. (It's part of the Act-Learn-Build-Repeat model I have talked about throughout.)

So, small setbacks = Good.

Large-scale failures = Bad

But there is one thing worse than large-scale failures—and that is not starting anything new at all. People can be extremely risk averse, and the idea of a venture not working out can scare them to the point where they never get underway. They keep thinking about the idea and/or doing more and more research, and they never pull the trigger. Or they don't start because their advisors are very conservative and keep pointing out reasons why they should delay, so they wait and think and refine and tweak and refine some more. Or they take too long to test the market, putting off actually beginning to the point where the competition has passed them by.

All of these situations are both depressing and unnecessary. As I have said before, if you think you have a good idea, get into the marketplace as quickly as you can, using as little money as possible, and see what happens. If it doesn't work, you can always regroup. But if you don't try you'll never know, and that is simply sad.

What Are We to Think?

Let end the chapter with three truisms.

- If you do exactly what everyone else does, you will never have a competitive edge. You will always be the same as everyone else.
- There are countless opportunities out there, if you can just figure out how to solve the market need.
- Solving those needs is difficult. And if you say, as most people do, "The challenge is too great for me," you will wind up with everyone else who didn't rise to the occasion—and you will never gain a competitive edge.

The people who succeed do more than the other guy. Sure, you can point to examples of people who got lucky—they chose the right parents and inherited wealth or position, or maybe they won some sort of lottery (genetic or actual)—but you never want to be in the position of having to rely on pure luck for your success.

That means if you want to stand out from the pack—which is how I define being successful—you need to welcome obstacles so that you can overcome them.

Takeaways for Entrepreneurs and the Rest of Us

1. If you are faced with a pleasant surprise, simply proceed down the path you were heading, although you might want to move a bit faster to make sure the opportunity window doesn't close. For example, if more people liked your idea than you could have imagined, continue executing but step up production, distribution, etc. to match heightened demand.

2. If you encounter an unwanted surprise, treat it as a gift and accept it wholeheartedly. It gives you new information, new evidence that your competition does not have. Solve the problem if you can. If you can't, see if it points to an opportunity or make it an asset (and build it into your offering).

3. Attitude is key. If you assume that everything, even the unexpected, is a gift, it will be.

CHAPTER 9

Getting Motivated and Staying Motivated for the Long Haul

Often, the biggest problem people have with achieving their goals is getting started. It seems that Sir Isaac Newton got it right with his first law of motion: bodies at rest tend to stay at rest. Many people just can't seem to get underway. They simply don't take action, and spend the rest of their lives talking about what might have been instead of what was.

So, what does it take to get started? One easy way is to have someone else light a fire under you—"If you don't do X, by such and such a time, you're fired"—or you light one under yourself—"I am not going to sleep tonight until I have taken a first step toward finding a new market for our product."

The problem with lighting a fire under yourself (or having it lit for you) is that eventually your backside gets burned. It's not a great long-term strategy. Once the threat ends, you have no real motivation to continue. And if you are operating in an environment where you are constantly threatened, you will get demoralized very quickly. (Think about what it was like—or would be like—to work for a boss who yelled at you all the time.)

So, what is the best way to get started? Identify:

- Something that you want.
- Something that you can do about that goal with the means at hand, i.e. taking an action that is within your level of acceptable loss. (The cost will be minimal, if the action doesn't work out. See the discussion in chapter 5.)

Put that way, there are only four logical explanations for why you would not move toward your goal:

1. Habit (you aren't used to moving toward your objective, so you don't).
2. You don't have the means at hand.
3. The perceived cost/risk is too high.
4. You are lying to yourself about what you want.

The fourth is rarely the case. Most people who say they want to get a new job or meet someone or lose weight or, in our case, want their product or service to succeed really do want to find new employment, find that significant other, be thinner, or find success with their business. As for habit, that's "simply" a matter of getting used to taking action. (More on that in a second.) So, that is not the likely cause for the delay either.

This means that if you aren't taking action toward what you want, you perceive the action as being either too costly or too risky. What's the solution? It seems simple, doesn't it? Reduce the cost and risk to acceptable levels so that you can get underway.

If it were as easy as all that, you would have done it. So you need some help. Here's one easy solution. Talk to a friend about the challenge you face: "I really want to start this company I have been dreaming of, but I just can't seem to get going."

> Action trumps everything.

Together, push the idea as far as you can. Figuring it out could take a couple of conversations, and that's fine. But don't wait until the end of all your talks to get moving. Remember, we want to make sure that habit—that you are in the a habit of *not moving* toward what you want—is *not* the problem. By the end of the first conversation, figure out the first small steps you can take to make your idea a reality and set a deadline—say, a week—for reporting back to your friend. At the next meeting, say what you did to follow up or explain why you didn't do anything.

Isn't setting a deadline the same as lighting a fire under yourself? Yes, but also no. It is similar in the sense that you have drawn a proverbial line in the sand. But no, because you are acknowledging up front that you may not take action.

Let's suppose you don't. At the next meeting with your friend, you explain why. Maybe it was because you were sick and so you give yourself a pass. But it could be you didn't take action because you found the idea of pitching potential prospects about your idea too intimidating, and stage fright won out over getting underway. If that's the case, you and your friend can break the next step into even smaller parts. For example, is there someone you know you could practice on, who would be able to give you an objective assessment of what you have? That could take some of the pressure off while at the same time advancing the ball a bit.

If that didn't work, you'd look for an even smaller step you could take. And so the process goes, until you reduce the next step to a point where it is doable.

Once You Are Underway

The need for motivation does not end once you are up and running. Sometimes, even if we have had some success, we can use a little help to keep going in the face of the inevitable obstacles we are going to encounter, no matter how experienced we are or how much we have accomplished.

Here are proven approaches that have worked for me, my friends who run business—both large firms and entrepreneurial ones—and others I have talked to. Let's run through them quickly, because some of these will resonate with you.

Necessity. A lot of my friends who are entrepreneurs are incredibly earnest and wouldn't romanticize love, let alone commerce, even if you pointed the proverbial gun to their heads. When asked what keeps them going, they talk about the mortgage that has to be paid or an elderly parent's medical bills they are responsible for. Says one, "John Wayne got it right. 'A man's got to do what a man's got to do.' And that applies to women, too." (I have to admit I could relate to this sentiment. At one point three of my kids were in private colleges at the same time. During those very expensive years, I took to saying, "I can't afford either writer's block or sloth." Knowing that the various bursars were going to be sending me bills was enough to keep me going no matter what impediments blocked my path.)

Quotes. Inspirational quotes were cited by many, but the ways they used them were as unique as they were. Some had a wall filled with quotes they had discovered through the years, while others took to taping a particular favorite (such as "Just keep swimming" from the kids' movie *Finding Nemo*) to their computer monitor, or they used it as a screensaver. If this sort of thing works for you, you can find lists of inspirational quotes just about everywhere you look. *Forbes* has a very good one as well. Google "list of inspirational quotes" and see what gets you fired up.

The knowledge that employees are relying on you. This is related to the necessity argument. A large number of entrepreneurs I talked to mentioned all the people who could potentially be out of work if they did less than their absolute best and their company suffered. Feeling responsible for their employees' economic future kept them going no matter what. Some thought about their employees in general while others focused on what the business going under would mean to one particular employee and his family, but just about every entrepreneur I interviewed commented on the impact her business failing would have on the people who worked for her.

Personal pride. It was hard to get people to admit to this one until they had a second (or third) glass of wine. But although they rarely talk about it publicly, many entrepreneurs are extremely proud of what they have accomplished and take (usually quiet) satisfaction in keeping the enterprise going no matter what problems come up along the way. They like the fact that they are the only one in the office at 6 a.m., working away at making their company better.

A mission to change the world. Not everyone was as evocative as Steve Jobs (who used to say, as a way of rallying Apple employees, "We are going to make insanely great products"), but a significant number of the entrepreneurs and businesspeople I talked to truly believe their offerings will make the world a better place. It is their deeply help belief in that mission that keeps them going. They know they are making a difference.

Support groups. This strategy provides benefits in one of two ways (and it is possible for one group to supply both). In option one, entrepreneurs meet periodically with other entrepreneurs who offer words of encouragement and advice when they're stuck. Among the entrepreneurs I spoke with who participated in this sort of group, the businesspeople who made up the support group were usually *not* in the same industry or even the same part of the country as the entrepreneur. The key thing was that it served as a meeting of peers. Even if an entrepreneur did not ask for, or need, advice, simply being associated with other successful people made those I talked with feel compelled to keep up, and that is the second advantage here. Not wanting to fall behind the others served as a motivating force.

They have a chip on their shoulder. More people than I would have thought say they keep going no matter what to prove to all the people "who told me I would never be successful that they were wrong." Intriguingly, this desire to "show them" continues even after the entrepreneur has become successful. Attaining success does not lessen this dynamic as a motivating force. The chip remains firmly in place.

Considering the alternative. This one, too, took two forms. To keep themselves going, some entrepreneurs thought back to the days before they started their companies and recalled how unhappy they were working for someone else. Others pictured what it would be like to once again have a boss. Either image, they said, was enough to keep them plugging away. This quote from one entrepreneur was representative: "The thought of going back to the cubicle farm is enough to keep me going no matter what problems I face running my own company."

A legacy. Knowing that their company may be the only real thing they are remembered for, or hoping that their kids will take over the business someday, keeps many entrepreneurs going when times get tough or they simply get tired. They feel compelled to leave something of lasting value behind.

Momentum. This one was cited by just about everyone I talked to. Goals like "We need to generate $1 million in sales within the first year" can sound awfully daunting from a standing start, because you are beginning with no revenues at all. And, obviously, if the objective seems impossible to achieve, you may never get underway. But if you say, "Let's get $83,333 coming in this month and $83,333 next month," the numbers don't seem as big and you get a chance to celebrate twelve small wins, as well as the one big one, when you hit $1 million in sales.

A diagnosis. Here's how one entrepreneur described this one for me: "You know when you are physically feeling lousy and know it is more than a cold or the flu, but you don't know what it is? Simply not knowing is worrisome. Once you get a diagnosis—even if it is something bad like pneumonia—you feel better because you know what it is and what you are up against. It is the same for me in my business. If I feel bad but if I get a friend, a peer—or even a shrink—to tell me what is going on, I feel better once I have a name for it. A diagnosis. That, in and of itself, is enough for me to come up with a battle plan to keep going. If I can name it, I can fight it."

Visualization. This one has never worked for me, although several of the people I talked to swear by it. They contend that focusing on what success will ultimately look like keeps them going. I worry that having a fixed image of success could either lead you to overlook or keep you from pursuing other opportunities you might encounter on the way, because they don't fit into your preconceived notion. Still, if visualization works for you, use it.

Exercise. Make sure that you move and think. Sometimes being tired, depressed, and wrung out is "simply" a matter of overwork or being out of shape (or both). When it comes to overwork, taking a break—at regular points—could be enough to keep you going.

As for exercise, at the very least, if you get into shape you will have more energy—even if your exercise program doesn't do a darn thing to improve your company's performance. There is no downside (and it will make you feel better physically).

Staying out of your own way. There will be enough circumstances beyond your control that could take the wind out of your sails, as my grandmother used to say. Don't make your life harder than it has to be. Simplify everything you can. (Leaving yourself ten minutes less than you need to get to the airport is never a good idea, for example.) Delegate the stuff you are bad at, and become as organized as humanly possible. Stress is the enemy of creativity. And creating more stress for yourself than you have to is simply dumb. Every time you encounter self-induced stress, figure out a way to eliminate it going forward.

A running score. This one is for all the hard-charging Type A's out there—that is, you. If you keep a running tally of the jobs you have completed, clients you've landed, and sales you've made since you first opened your doors, you'll be motivated as you see the numbers increase—and you'll want them to increase further. Just looking at the scoreboard and knowing that you need to get the numbers higher can keep you fired up.

A mantra. Keep telling yourself that the best way to predict the future is to create it. And then go create it.

Learn from Mistakes

You've seen this movie. Someone, maybe you, has worked passionately and for an extended period of time to develop what he *knows* is a wonderful product or service. The big day comes and he launches it with incredibly high expectations, feeling assured that everyone will see just how good it is.

And nothing happens. The product or service sinks without a trace.

How does the creator react? He blames the market. "The audience couldn't see the brilliance of what we had. People are stupid. It's their fault. We did everything right." And absolutely no learning takes place. Presented this way, the entrepreneur's attitude sounds ridiculous, right? And yet that reaction happens every single day.

The only person who gets to decide whether you have a truly great product is your customers. If they love it, you do. If they don't, you don't. And if they don't buy what you were trying to sell them, you need to figure out why; otherwise, you run the very real risk of making the same mistake next time you introduce something new.

Now, you could be right. Perhaps it was a great product. But it may have been one that solved no real need. Or maybe it solved a need but you didn't communicate it clearly enough. Or maybe it solved a need and the communication was good but...

Whatever that "but" is, you need to (1) understand it and (2) work hard not to repeat that mistake the next time. I know it sounds simple. I also know from personal experience that it is not. I can be as guilty of this lack of learning problem as anyone else.

Many years ago, however, I realized how beneficial it can be to learn from mistakes, and as counterintuitive as it sounds, those mistakes can serve as a wonderful motivating force. Let me tell you the story. Carl Sewell, one of the nation's smartest retailers, and I were just about finished writing a book about how customer service can be a very effective business strategy—a radical idea back in the late 1980s. As we finished up for the day, Carl asked what he thought was the world's most basic question: "When do we focus group what we have?"

Book publishers don't like to run focus groups. The editors and salespeople think they know exactly what their readers are looking for. Writers (like me) suffer from this egotism, too. "But how will we ever know what people want if we don't ask them?"

Carl responded logically when I told him all this. If the publisher wouldn't hold a focus group, he would pay for it himself. He hired a big-deal research firm and told them to give the first one hundred pages of our manuscript to a representative sample of our potential audience.

A couple of weeks later, twelve people sat around a conference table with a moderator while Carl, our editor, and I looked on from the other side of a two-way mirror. The participants were told we were there. As you will see, it did not inhibit them one whit.

The group began by discussing my proposed title. I knew we had to call the book *The $332,000 Customer*. (The number is what average customers spent with Sewell at one of his car dealerships over their lifetime.) My title, I argued humbly, was intriguing, thought provoking, and would make the book jump off the shelves. (I cannot begin to tell you how clever I thought I was with that title.)

Within seconds, it was clear that the group was split about how smart I was. Nine out of the twelve people thought it was absolutely the worst title they had ever heard. The other three said they had heard worse, but they agreed my title was terrible.

It went downhill from there. They loved our central argument, but couldn't we reorganize things somehow to make the information within the book easier to use? They liked the idea of checklists at the end of each chapter, but couldn't we tell them what they should do about what they just read, and why did the book need to be so wordy? And so it went.

After a couple of days of licking our wounds, we took the comments to heart. We came up with a new title. What kept resonating was that the focus group thought—correctly—that the entire book was about capturing a customer and then keeping him forever. Since the fundamental idea was so important to them, we ended up using it twice: *Customers for Life: How to Turn That One-Time Buyer into a Lifetime Customer.*

To make the book easier to digest, I chopped long chapters into two or three shorter ones and made the book completely modular, so readers could skip the stuff that wasn't relevant to them. And I took out every show-offy turn of phrase I could find and used nothing but short sentences with active verbs. The changes worked. The book is a key reason my kids were able to go to the colleges of their choice.

Painful as it was to hear the focus group tell me all the mistakes I made in the initial draft of *Customers for Life*, the process ended up being hugely beneficial. I have kept the lessons I learned at the forefront of my mind in everything I have written ever since.

I don't like making mistakes. No one does. But when I do, emulating the most successful people I know, I work really hard to learn from them. And that is the moral here: learn from your mistakes. Having things go wrong—you don't get the sale, the client hates your solution to their problem—is enough to demotivate anyone (if that is a word). You are going to feel bad. Accept that. And give yourself a *short* period to wallow. Then learn from what went wrong. That way, you will be turning the rejection into something you can benefit from. It sounds simplistic—though of course it is difficult to do—and clichéd. But it is true. And more importantly, it does work.

You don't have to look much further than the creator of *Dilbert* to see the proof in that statement. Scott Adams captured the idea in his book title *How to Fail at Almost Everything and Still Win Big: Kind of the Story of My Life*. Adams devotes an entire chapter to all the ventures he has been associated with that failed, and it is an impressive list. They include a meditation guide, several inventions, a number of computer games and software programs, and even—pre-*Dilbert*—a new type of file folder.

But Adams says he is grateful for his failures. Through each one he learned new skills and made contacts and gained experience, all of which he drew on when creating his comic strip. Why failure is good is a major theme in this sort of memoir. As Adams writes: "Failure is your friend. It is the raw material of success. Invite it in. Learn from it. And don't let it leave until you pick its pocket."

Sounds like a solid approach to me.

Simplify

I used to make my own bread. It's not that I particularly like to bake—it's okay, but I don't find the emotional fulfillment in it that some people do—I did it because I couldn't get good bread where I lived. I now spend about half my life in and around Manhattan, an area of the country where good bread is an art form. I no longer bake.

My ice cream maker is collecting dust. Ditto that pasta maker. I've found that there are people who can do what I used to and do it better, or at least as well as me, and so my time could better be spent on more productive things. It took me a long time to start doing this in my business.

Of course, I know the owner is supposed to concentrate on only the most essential stuff. But:

A. I can do the nonessential work in my business far faster than most people.
B. I hate having outstanding things lingering. So, I figure I will do what needs to be done—even if it isn't the sort of thing I should be doing—and get it out of the way. Then I'll go back to my work after that. Dumb, I know, but that is how I am hardwired (and you may be wired this way, too).

Let me tell you how I have gotten better about this using a real example. I am working on a complicated project for the company that is now my biggest client. I did a solid piece of work on a particular segment, and while the client liked it, he had some revisions he wanted to make.

I looked at his suggested revisions and realized the rework could essentially be divided into two parts. There was about an hour needed to tweak his ideas—which were surprisingly good, and my fiddling with them could make them even better—and then about six hours of scut work. Much of that work entailed a whole lot of copyediting and revising of Excel spreadsheets to accommodate all the changes the client had made. It wouldn't be hard, but it would be time consuming. That's where that six-hour figure came from.

Before, I would have just done everything myself over the weekend. But I am trying to get better about this and so I delegated the scut work. Instead, I spent those six hours last weekend when I otherwise would have used playing with Excel, creating two proposals that could generate about $150,000 in new business.

Now, I wish I could say that passing on the relatively mindless work was easy for me. It wasn't. The client sent me the revisions on Thursday and I could have had everything done forty-eight hours later. While I tweaked his ideas to improve them late Thursday, I won't have the rest of the work back from the person I delegated to for another week. It doesn't screw up the deadline. We will be fine. But it will still take a week longer than if I had done the work myself.

Knowing that I got the two proposals for new business out the door makes me feel good. But the bigger takeaway for me is that every time I am about to do something that really could be handled by someone else—even if I have to outsource and pay for it—I am going to ask, "Is this the absolute best use of my time?" Working efficiently and at the things you are best at may be the best form of motivation there is.

Takeaways for Entrepreneurs and the Rest of Us

1. **When it comes to obstacles, your attitude and mind-set are probably the most important things.** There is a wonderful quote from Henry Ford: "Whether you think you can, or whether you think you can't, you're right."

2. When times get tough, focusing on your end goal can help keep you going. Every day, as you know, is not going to be a walk in the park, so be prepared for setbacks and adopt specific strategies to stay motivated.

3. Keep things as simple as you can. Fewer moving parts means less can go wrong.

AFTERWORD

Being an Entrepreneur Is Less Scary Than You Think

The host of a Midwestern talk show who was interviewing me ran out of questions about a blog entry I had posted on *Inc.* so she invited questions from listeners. The third person who called in began this way: "I think I have a good idea for a company, but I am scared to death about starting. Any advice for me on how I can overcome my fear?"

It was too bad we only had ten minutes left, as I could have gone on much longer. This is one of my favorite topics. There are countless people (the number is probably in the millions) who have an idea for creating a business—either for themselves or for their employer—and yet they have done nothing about it. Why haven't they? My guess is that the primary reason is they don't have the requisite desire, as we talked about throughout.

But the second biggest reason, I am convinced, is that they are like the person who called in. They are afraid. What do I tell these people? My starting point is always this: I don't know if fear is helpful as a motivating force, as many people have argued, but I do know it is normal.

Venturing into the unknown—and that is exactly what you are doing every time you start something new—is by definition scary. That fact may be the biggest reason so many *don't* start anything new, despite having the requisite desire. They are frozen in place by their fear, and that fear of the unknown keeps them from beginning.

The primary cause of this fear is the very real possibility that you may fail. And that fear, in turn, has three parts.

1. **You fear that because your idea failed—or might fail—you are, or will be, a failure.** And who wants to view herself that way? The guaranteed way to not fail is to not try.
2. **You worry about what other people will think** if your new venture doesn't work out.
3. **You are afraid of the lasting consequences** that could come from failure. There is a very real fear that not only will you use up valuable resources—money, time, and reputation capital—but you will have jeopardized your current status and position in the attempt as well.

As I said, these fears are natural. But saying the fear is natural is not particularly helpful, nor does it give you a plan to eliminate it. I think this can help: when we think of this fear, we are usually imagining a full-blown venture that hasn't worked out. We picture ourselves having invested hundreds of hours and untold amounts of money to get our idea up and running. And if that were the case, the failure would certainly be devastating.

But you don't have to approach starting anything new that way. Let's use a couple of extreme examples to hammer home the point. You could quit your day job to see if you can turn your hobby of building birdhouses into a full-fledged business. Or, you could build a few and take them to local craft fairs and post pictures of them on a retail site like Etsy or eBay and see if anyone is interested. If they don't sell, it is no big deal. You are not out very much in either time or money. And if they do sell, you can take another small step toward making Birdhouses 'R' Us a reality. Maybe you think about selling your birdhouse plans as well as the finished houses, or you hire a retired neighbor to build them for you.

Similarly, starting a new pizza joint from scratch at Fourth and Main could cost hundreds of thousands of dollars and take months, and you would take a substantial hit if it failed. But how much time would it take to survey potential customers and give away samples of what you plan to offer, to see if you are on to something? If people don't like what you have, or if they tell you they are really happy with the pizza place two blocks down, your "failure" is small.

The idea here is simple. Breaking your ideas for something new into extremely small steps diminishes the risk and thus (hopefully) the fear as well. It also gives you early confirmation that you are on to something, or it could reveal that you need to do more work.

There are three other benefits to taking this approach.

1. You can get started right away. No elaborate planning is needed. You take a small step and see how the market reacts.
2. You don't need a lot of resources to take that small step.
3. You can respond quickly to market needs.

What we have just explored in depth works for established entrepreneurs as well. Just because you have succeeded once doesn't mean you won't have fears when you try for an encore. Taking small steps should help.

This Should Sound Familiar

If everything we just talked about sounds familiar—it should. It is nothing more than a blown-out version of the first step in the Act-Learn-Build-Repeat model that we discussed in chapter 1.

We are talking about the best way to start. And if you break starting into extremely small steps, the risk of taking each one becomes smaller. If the risk is smaller, it is less scary and you are more likely to begin.

Begin.

ACKNOWLEDGMENTS

Whether it ends up being in a well-respected blog, newspaper, magazine, or book, there is no greater job on earth than writing nonfiction. You literally get to go around the world and ask people questions, many of which are none of your business, and almost always people give you thoughtful answers.

With that by way of background, I want to thank everyone who is quoted (even if they traded candor for anonymity) within the book for their time and intelligence.

And I would like to also thank Steve Forbes and Tom Post at *Forbes* and Eric Schurenberg and Lindsay Blakely at *Inc.* for letting me play with the genesis of these ideas on their dime and invariably making them better.

NOTES

Chapter 4

1. At one time, there were more than a thousand Howard Johnson restaurants in the United States, and by 1965, HoJo's had sales that were more than those of McDonald's, Burger King, and Kentucky Fried Chicken combined. At the time, Howard Johnson's served more food than anyone in the world except the United States Army.

Chapter 6

1. "Startup Financing—How Much? From Whom?" Growthology: A Blog of the Kauffman Foundation, September 6, 2012, http://www.growthology.org/growthology/2012/09/startup-financing-how-much-from-whom.html.
2. It is not just books, of course. Entrepreneurial finance is now a standard offering at the nation's business schools. The following listing from Harvard is representative:

   "Entrepreneurial Finance is primarily designed for students who plan to get involved with a new venture at some point in their career—as a founder, early employee, advisor or investor. However, the course is also appropriate for students interested in gaining a broader view of the financing landscape for young firms, going beyond the basics of venture capital and angel financing to look at venture debt, bank finance, corporate venture capital and receivables financing."

INDEX

Index

Index

Index

ABOUT THE AUTHOR

A long-time contributor to *The New York Times*, Paul B. Brown has written, co-written and "ghosted" numerous business book best-sellers including *Customers for Life* (with Carl Sewell) that has been translated into nineteen different languages and has been updated twice since its publication in 1990.

Paul is a former writer and editor for *Businessweek*, *Financial World*, and *Forbes*.

He is a graduate of Rutgers College and Rutgers University Law School and is a member of both the New Jersey and Massachusetts bars, but he asks that you don't hold that against him.